MW01015451

DATE
WITH
NUMBERS

2000+ INTERESTING EQUATIONS EXPRESSING
EACH DATE OF THE YEAR

VIKAS OMPRAKASH GOYAL

INDIA · SINGAPORE · MALAYSIA

Notion Press

Old No. 38, New No. 6
McNichols Road, Chetpet
Chennai - 600 031

First Published by Notion Press 2019
Copyright © Vikas Omprakash Goyal 2019
All Rights Reserved.

ISBN 978-1-64587-874-2

Dedication

To my father who invoked the love of logic in me

To my mother who nourished in me her values

To my wife who has completed me with her love

And to my son who will always be my inspiration

Contents

A Note from the Author

Having lost my father at the age of 12, I began teaching mathematics to support my education. What began as survival ultimately turned into a lifelong journey and passion for guiding students, parents, and professionals upon the nuances of this subject.

The objective of this book is to bring out the beauty of numbers by linking it to dates. Dates are special, and they are universal; birthdays, marriage anniversary, work anniversary or even the paycheck day – dates are meaningful to us. We remember and celebrate these dates each year. Through these very dates, this book expresses each of the 365 days of the year using basic mathematics.

The book ignites the curious minds of all ages by blending the beauty of numeric logic with the emotions of dates. It takes you on a never-before journey with math, where every day is a new opportunity to learn how simple math can be.

With this book, every day will be a date with numbers.

January

1st January

1st January can be expressed as 1/1

$11 = 2^4 - 2^3 + 2^2 - 2^1 + 2^0$

11 is the first 2-digit prime number

$11^2 = 5 * 4 * 3 * 2 * 1 + 1 = 5! + 1$

(One of the three Brown numbers)

$11^2 = 121$ is a palindrome and so is

$11^3 = 1331$

$11^4 = 14641$

By applying 4 straight cuts, a pizza can be cut in 11 pieces

2nd January

2nd January can be expressed as 2/1

21 is the sum of first 3 even power of 2

$21 = 2^0 + 2^2 + 2^4$

21 is the sum of first 6 natural numbers

$21 = 1 + 2 + 3 + 4 + 5 + 6$

$21 = (4^1 + 4^2 + 4^3)/4$

The number (21) in base 10 when converted to base 2 becomes 10101 (Palindrome)

$(21)_{10} = (10101)_2$

When converted to base 4 becomes 111

$(21)_{10} = (111)_4$

When converted to base 19 gets interchanged to 12

$(21)_{10} = (12)_{19}$

3rd January

Birthdate 31 (3/1) is Prime

31 – That's the exact number of days in the month of January

$31 = 2^0 + 2^1 + 2^2 + 2^3 + 2^4$

$31 = 3^3 + 3^1 + 3^0 = 27 + 3 + 1$

The sum of digits of square of 31 is square of the sum of digits of 31

$31^2 = 961 = 9 + 6 + 1 = 16$

$(3 + 1)^2 = (9 + 6 + 1) = 16$

Cube-root of 31 is 3.14; which is approximate value of Pi

31 is prime and so are the following

331

3,331

33,331

3,33,331

33,33,331

3,33,33,331

The number (31) in base 10 when converted to base 2 becomes 11111

$(31)_{10} = (11111)_2$

When converted to base 5 becomes 111

$(31)_{10} = (111)_5$

When converted to base 28 gets interchanged to 13

$(31)_{10} = (13)_8$

4th January

Birthdate 41 (4/1) is Prime

41 is the sum of first 6 prime

41 = 2 + 3 + 5 + 7 + 11 + 13

Both birthdate and birth month are perfect squares individually. Probability of occurrence of such numbers is only 4.1% (15 favourable outcomes out of 365)

$41 = 3^0 + 3^0 + 3^1 + 3^2 + 3^3$

$41 = 4^{(1+1)} + (4+1)^{(1+1)} = 16 + 25$

The reciprocal of 41 is 1/41 forms a pattern of 5 digits getting repeated

1/41 = 0.0243902439

$(41)_{10} = (41)_{18} + (41)_{35}$

5th January

5th January can be expressed as 5/1

$51 = 5^{(1+1)} + 5^{(1+1)} + 1^5$

$51 = 26 + 25 = 26^2 - 25^2$

$51 = (1! * 3!) + (2! * 4!)$

51 in base 2 is Palindrome

$(51)_{10} = (110011)_2$

Also 51 is 123 in Base 6

$(51)_{10} = (123)_6$

6th January

6th January can be expressed as 6/1

$61 = 3^4 - 3^3 + 3^2 - 3^1 + 3^0$

61 is a prime number

$61 = 6^2 + (6 - 1)^2$

$61 = (6 - 1)^3 - (6 - 2)^3$

61, when rolled upside down become 19 which is also prime

Sum of first 61 natural numbers

$1 + 2 + 3 + ... + 61 = 1861$

1861 when turn upside down becomes 1681 which is perfect square of 41

7th January

7th January can be expressed as 7/1

71 is a prime number

71 is sum of three consecutive primes

71 = 19 + 23 + 29

$71^2 = 7! + 1 = 5141 = 5040 + 1$

(Known as Brown number)

$71^3 = 357911 \rightarrow$ Pattern 3, 5, 7, 9 and 11

8th January

8th January can be expressed as 8/1

1/81 = 0.12345679012345679

Square of 81 ends in 61 and Cube of 61 ends in 81

$81^2 = 6561$ and $61^3 = 226981$

$81 = (8 + 1)^{(1 + 1)}$

81 which is perfect square of 9 becomes perfect square of 10 in base 9,

$(81)_{10} = (100)_9$

Perfect square of 11 in base 8,

$(81)_{10} = (121)_8$

Perfect square of 12 in base 7 and

$(81)_{10} = (144)_7$

Perfect square of 100 in base 3

$(81)_{10} = (10000)_3$

9th January

9th January can be expressed as 9/1

91 = sum of first 13 natural numbers

91 = 13 + 12 + 11 + ... + 1

$91 = 1^2 + 2^2 + 3^2 + 4^2 + 5^2 + 6^2$

$91 = 3^3 + 4^3$

$91^2 = 8281$ and if we add all digits of 8 + 2 + 8 + 1 = 19 i.e reverse of 91

If we write down all natural numbers till 91 the sum will be 4186.

The sum of whose digits is 4 + 1 + 8 + 6 = 19 i.e. reverse of 91

+91 is the ISD code for India

10th January

10th January can be expressed as 10/1

101 is the first 3-digit prime number

101 is prime and palindrome

101 is the only prime of form $10^n + 1$

101 is sum of 5 consecutive primes

101 = 13 + 15 + 17 + 19 + 23

11th January

11th January can be expressed as 11/1

Square of 111 is a palindrome, so is its cube, 4th power and 5th power

111 * 111 = 12321

1111 * 1111 = 1234321

11111 * 11111 = 123454321...

111 * 111 * 111 = 13673631

1/111 = 0.009009009

12th January

12th January can be expressed as 12/1

121 can be expressed using its own digits (Friedman number)

$121 = 11^2$

$121 = (1 + 2)^0 + (1 + 2)^1 + (1 + 2)^2 + (1 + 2)^3 + (1 + 2)^4$

$121 = 3^0 + 3^1 + 3^2 + 3^3 + 3^4$

(Only Square of this form)

$121^2 = 14641$ which is palindrome

121 = 5! + 1 = 5 * 4 * 3 * 2 * 1 + 1

(Brocard Conjecture)

121 Seconds = 2 Minutes 1 Seconds

13th January

13th January can be expressed as 13/1

131 is a prime number

113 is a prime

So is 311 (permutable prime)

Embedded Prime – 3 is prime, 13 is prime 31 is prime

131 = 41 + 43 + 47 (Sum of all prime in 40's)

$131 = (1 + 3 + 1)^3 + (1! + 3! + 1!)$

14th January

14th January can be expressed as 14/1

141 = sum of squares of 13 (14 – 1) natural numbers

First three digits of square of 2 is 1.41

15th January

15th January can be expressed as 15/1

151 is a prime number and so its sum of digits (5 + 1 + 1) = 7 and (1 * 5 * 1) = 5 is prime

151 is prime in base 2, 3, 4 and 5

$(151)_{10} = (10010111)_2$

$(151)_{10} = (12121)_3$

$(151)_{10} = (2113)_4$

$(151)_{10} = (1101)_5$

$151 = 5^0 + 5^2 + 5^3$

16th January

16th January can be expressed as 16/1

161 = 23 * 7 and

23 − 7 = 16 which is birth date

161 when rotated upside down it becomes 191. 161 and 191 both are prime

17th January

17th January can be expressed as 17/1

If we represent 171 as abc, then ab, ac and bc all are prime

171 = 1 + 2 + 3 + 4 + ... + 18

Sum of first 18 natural numbers

Cube root of 5 is approximately 1.71

Sum of digits of 171 = 1 + 7 + 1 = 9

If we write all numbers starting from 1 to 171 the sum comes to 14706. The sum of its digit is 1 + 4 + 7 + 0 + 6 = 18 = 1 + 8 = 9

The square of 171 is 29241 and if we add all digits of 2 + 9 + 2 + 4 + 1 = 18 = 1 + 8 = 9

22nd January

22nd January can be expressed as 22/1

$221^2 = 48841$

By reversing LHS, RHS gets reversed

$122^2 = 14884$

Power of 2, 3 and 4 of 221 ends in 41, 61 and 81

If you write down first 221 natural numbers and add them

$1 + 2 + 3 + ... + 221 = 24531$ (Number consisting of 1, 2, 3, 4 and 5)

23rd January

23rd January can be expressed as 23/1

$1 + 2 + 3 + ... + 21 = 231$

$231 = 11 + 22 + 33 + 44 + 55 + 66$

6 has four factors 1, 2, 3 and 4. If we take only 1, 2, 3 and add them we get $1 + 2 + 3 = 6$ which is first perfect number

$231^4 = 2847396321$. It terminates in 321

24th January

24th January can be expressed as 24/1

241 is prime and so it's sum of digits is: $2 + 4 + 1 = 7$

$241 = 15^0 + 15^1 + 15^2$

Cube root of 14 is 2.41

24th January, when written as 24/01 becomes 2401 which is perfect square of 49 which is again perfect square of 7.

7 is the sum of digits of 2401 = 2 + 4 + 0 + 1 = 7

241 = 170 + 017 (Sum of 170 and it's reverse)

25th January

25th January can be expressed as 25/1

$251 = 2^3 + 3^3 + 6^3$

$251 = 2 * 5^{(1+2)} + 1$

$251^2 = 63,001$

$251^3 = 15813251$. It ends in 251

Cube root of 16 is 2.51

$2501 = 50^2 + 1$ (Friedman Number)

26th January

Birth date 26 is between a perfect square and perfect cube. Only one such number exists

26th January can be expressed as 26/01

2601 is a perfect square of 51

27th January

27th January can be expressed as 27/1

271 is a prime number and the first 3 digits of value of exponential e = 2.71

271 can be expressed in powers of 3

$271 = 3^0 + 3^3 + 3^5 = 1 + 27 + 243 = 271$

$271^2 = 73,441$

If we take sum of digits of 73,441 it becomes 7 + 3 + 4 + 4 + 1 = 19 = 1 + 9 = 10 = 1 + 0 = 1

$271^3 = 19902511$

If we take sum of digits of 19902511, it becomes 1 + 9 + 9 + 0 + 2 + 5 + 1 + 1 = 28 = 2 + 8 = 10 = 1 + 0 = 1

If we write down all the numbers starting from 1 + 2 + 3 + ... + 271 = 36856

If we take the sum of digits of 36856, it becomes 3 + 6 + 8 + 5 + 6 = 28 = 2 + 8 = 10 = 1 + 0 = 1

1/271 = 0.0036900369...

271 = 180 + 81

$271 = 4^2 + 5^2 + 6^2 + 7^2 + 8^2 + 9^2$

28th January

28th January can be expressed as 28/1

$281 \rightarrow 2 = 2^1, 8 = 2^3$ and $2 = 2^1$

Sum of first 14 primes is 281

$281 = 2 + 3 + 5 + ... + 43$

The product of digits gives a perfect square = $2 * 8 * 1 = 16$

Birthdate * birth month is 28 (28 * 1)

28 is the second perfect number

$281 = 190 + 091$

4 different square consists of 5 digits: 1, 6, 7, 8 and 9

$281^2 = 78961$

$137^2 = 18769,$

$133^2 = 17689,$

$286^2 = 81796$

29th January

29th January can be expressed as 29/1

$291 = (50 + 47) * (50 - 47)$

$4700^2 + 291^2 = 4709^2$

30th January

30th January can be expressed as 30/1

$301 = (4 + 3) * 43$

$301 = 3^4 - 43 + 1$

301 is sum of three primes out of which one is palindrome

$301 = 97 + 101 + 103$

31st January

31st January can be expressed as 31/1

311 is the prime number. If we reverse the digits, i.e 113 its still prime. Also 131 is prime

If we write 311 as abc, then ab, bc and ac are prime. 31, 11, and 31 are all prime

If we add all the digits of 311 – 3 + 1 + 1 = 5, that's prime too

More if we multiply 311 = 3 * 1 * 1. It's prime too

311 can be expressed as sum of 3 primes – 101 + 103 + 17

311 can also be expressed as sum of 11 primes –

11 + 13 + 17 + 19 + 23 + 29 + 31 + 37 + 41 + 43 + 47

February

1st February

1st February can be expressed as 1/2

$12 = (1 + 2)^1 + (1 + 2)^2$

Sum of digits of 12 = 1 + 2 = 3 is prime

Product of digits of 12 = 1 * 2 = 2 is prime

$12^2 = 144$ and if we reverse 12 to get 21

$21^2 = 441$

The number of months is 12

1st February is 32nd day of the calendar year and there are 333 more days left in the calendar year

2nd February

2nd February can be expressed as 2/2

$22 = 1^4 + 2^3 + 3^2 + 4^1$

Sum of digits of 2 + 2 is a perfect square

Product of digits of 2 * 2 = 4 is perfect square again

Division of digits 2/2 = 1 is again a perfect square

$22^2 = 484$ which is palindrome

By applying 7 straight cuts, a pizza can be cut in 22 pieces. 22/7 is the approximate value of pi

3rd February

3rd February can be expressed as 3/2

$32 = 1^1 + 2^2 + 3^3$

$32 = 2^{(3+2)}$

Cube root of 32 is 3.2

$32^4 = 1048576$ – That's the number of rows in Microsoft Excel

32 is 1A in base system 22. First positive integer and 1st alphabet

$(32)_{10} = (1A)_{22}$

4th February

4th February can be expressed as 4/2

$42 = (0!)^2 + (1!)^2 + (3!)^2$

Birthday is square of birth month which has occurrence probability of 1.4%

If we multiply the birthday with birth-month we get 8 which is the number of alphabets in the month of February

$402 = 2^1 + 2^4 + 2^7 + 2^8$

5th February

5th February can be expressed as 5/2

$52 = 5^2 + 2^3$

$52 = (2!)^4 + (3!)^2$

52: Both digits are individually prime (5 and 2)

Sum of the digits is also prime (5 + 2)

Cube root of 141 is 5.2

6th February

6th February can be expressed as 6/2

$62 = 1^2 + 5^2 + 6^2$

$62 = 2^2 + 3^2 + 7^2$

$62 = 2^1 + 2^2 + 2^3 + 2^4 + 2^5$

62 in base 10 is 26 in base 28

$(62)_{10} = (26)_{28}$

7th February

7th February can be expressed as 7/2

$72 = 2^3 * 3^2$

As $72 = n(n + 1) = 8 * 9 =$ sum of first 8 consecutive even numbers $= 2 + 4 + 6 + 8 + 10 + 12 + 14 + 16$

$72 = 24 * 3$ and reverse of 72 is $27 = 24 + 3$

Sum of digits of $72 = 7 + 2 = 9$

Sum of digits of $72^2 = 5184 = 5 + 1 + 8 + 4 = 18 = 1 + 8 = 9$

Sum of digits of $72^3 = 373248 = 3 + 7 + 3 + 2 + 4 + 8 = 27$
$= 2 + 7 = 9$

Sum of digits of 72^4 = 26873856 = 2 + 6 + 8 + 7 + 3 + 8 + 5 + 6 = 45 = 4 + 5 = 9

72 is the pulse rate of human body at normal rate

8th February

Birthdate 8/2 (82) is special

$82 = 8^0 + (8 + 1)^2$

82^2 = 6,724. If we take sum of digits of 6,724 it becomes 6 + 7 + 2 + 4 = 19 = 1 + 9 = 10 = 1 + 0 = 1

82^3 = 551368. If we take sum of digits of 551368, it becomes 5 + 5 + 1 + 3 + 6 + 8 = 28 = 2 + 8 = 10 = 1 + 0 = 1

If we write down all the numbers starting from 1 + 2 + 3 + ... + 82 = 3403

If we take the sum of digits of 3403, it becomes 3 + 4 + 0 + 3 = 10 = 1 + 0 = 1

82 when converted to base system 7, it becomes 145

$(82)_{10} = (145)_7$

145 = 1! + 4! + 5!

9th February

9th February can be expressed as 9/2

$92 = 1 * 23 * 4$

92 when converted to base 8 becomes 134

$(92)_{10} = (134)_8$

$92 = 1^3 + 3^3 + 4^3 = 1 + 27 + 64$

$92 = 1^2 + 1^2 + 2^2 + 3^2 + 4^2 + 5^2 + 6^2$

$92 = 4! * 4 - 4$

10th February

10th February can be expressed as 10/2

$102 = 10^2 + 2$

$102^2 = 10404$

By reversing LHS, RHS gets reversed

$201^2 = 40401$

$102 = 5! - 4! + 3!$

$102 = 1^2 + 4^2 + 6^2 + 7^2$

$102 = 2^2 + 3^2 + 5^2 + 8^2$

11th February

11th February can be expressed as 11/2

$112 = 11^2 - (2 + 1)^2$

$112^2 = 12544$

$221^2 = 44521$

$112 = 1 * 2 + 2 * 3 + 3 * 4 + 4 * 5 + 5 * 6$

12th February

12th February can be expressed as 12/2

$122 = 11^{(1+1)} + 1$

122 is 145 in base 9 which is a Factorion

$(122)_{10} = (145)_9$

$145 = 1! + 4! + 5!$

$122 = 115 + 1 + 1 + 5$

$122^2 = 14884$

$221^2 = 48841$

$122 = 2^6 + 2^5 + 2^4 + 2^3 + 2^1 = 64 + 32 + 16 + 8 + 2$

13th February

13th February can be expressed as 13/2

$132 = 11 * 3 * 2^2$

$132 = (2^1 + 2^2 + 2^3 + 2^4 + 2^5 + 2^6) + (3 * 2 * 1)$

$132 = 13 + 32 + 21 + 31 + 23 + 12$ (Digit reassembly number)

$132 = 22 + 44 + 66$

$132 = 2 * (1 + 2 + 3) * 11$

$132 = 2 * 11 + 2 * 22 + 2 * 33$

$132 = (13 - 1)^2 - (13 - 1)$

$132 = 22 + 20 + 18 + 16 + 14 + 12 + 10 + 8 + 6 + 4 + 2$

14th February

14th February can be expressed as 14/2

$1/142 = 0.007$

$142 = 2^{(14/2)} + 14$

$1 = 2^0, 4 = 2^2$ and $2 = 2^1$

$1 * 4 * 2$ = Perfect Cube

$1 + 4 + 2$ = Prime

15th February

15th February can be expressed as 15/2

$152 = 5! + 2^5$

$152 = 5^2 + 2^0 + 2^1 + 2^2 + 2^3 + 2^4 + 2^5 + 2^6$

$152^2 = 23,104$ (Square consisting of first 5 whole numbers)

$152 = 3^3 + 5^3$

16th February

16th February can be expressed as 16/2

Only possible date where DD is (M)^4

162 Can be expressed using first 4 natural number once

$162 = 2^1 * 3\char`^4$

$162 = 3 * 6 * 9$

17th February

17th February can be expressed as 17/2

Sum of digits of 172 = 1 + 7 + 2 = 10 = 1 + 0 = 1

Sum of digits of 172^2 = 29584 = 2 + 9 + 5 + 8 + 4 = 28 = 2 + 8 = 10 = 1 + 0 = 1

Sum of digits of 172^3 = 5088448 = 5 + 0 + 8 + 8 + 4 + 4 + 8 = 37 = 3 + 7 = 10 = 1 + 0 = 1

Sum of digits of 172^4 = 875213056 = 8 + 7 + 5 + 2 + 1 + 3 + 0 + 5 + 6 = 37 = 3 + 7 = 10 = 1 + 0 = 1

If we write down all the digits from 1 to 172 digits and add them, it becomes 14878

1 + 2 + 3 + ... + 172 = 14878

If we add all digits of 14878 = 1 + 4 + 8 + 7 + 8 = 28 = 2 + 8 = 10 = 1 + 0 = 1

18th February

18th February can be expressed as 18/2

$182 = 14^2 - 14^1$

182 = 18 + 82 + 28 + 12 + 21 + 21

182 is 222 in base 9 and 20202 in base 3

$(182)_{10} = (222)_9$

$(182)_{10} = (20202)_3$

19th February

19th February can be expressed as 19/2

192 is a happy number

$1^2 + 9^2 + 2^2 = 86$

$8^2 + 6^2 = 100$

$1^2 + 0^2 + 0^2 = 1$

$192 = (2^7 + 2^8)/2$

192 is the smallest number having 14 divisors

Cube root of 192 is approximately 5.76

5.76 is a perfect square of 2.4

$192^3 = 7077888$ consists only of 3 digits

20th February

20th February can be expressed as 20/2

$202 = (2 + 3 + 5 + 7)^2 - (2^2 + 3^2 + 5^2 + 7^2)$

202 is a palindrome and so is it's square

$202^2 = 40804$

$202 = 2^5 + 3^4 + 4^3 + 5^2$

21st February

21st February can be expressed as 21/2

The digits of 212's square are individually perfect square

212^2 = 44944

Also, palindrome both ways

212^3 = 9528128 ends in 8128 which is a perfect number

212^4 = 2019963136... begins with 2019 (Current year)

212 when written in base 3 becomes 21212

$(212)_{10} = (21212)_3$

22nd February

22nd February can be expressed as 22/2

$222 = 2^1 + 2^2 + 2^3 + 2^4 + 2^6 + 2^7$

$222 = (2 + 2 + 2)^3 + (2 + 2 + 2)$

$222 = (3!)^3 + 3!$

222 – Probability of having birthdate in DD/M where DD = M is only 0.55% (11/1 is the only possible number)

222 when written in binary becomes 11010100. If we add the digits

$(222)_{10} = (11010100)_2$

2 + 2 + 2 = 6 = 1 + 1 + 0 + 1 + 0 + 1 + 0 + 0

23rd February

23rd February can be expressed as 23/2

232 = 4^4 − 4!

232 = 6^3 + 2^4

24th February

24th February can be expressed as 24/2

242 = [(2 + 4 + 2)/3]^5 − 1

242 = 3^5 − 3^0

242 = 44 + 55 + 66 + 77

25th February

25th February can be expressed as 25/2

252 = 30240/120 = (10 * 9 * 8 * 7 * 6)/(5 * 4 * 3 * 2 * 1)

252 = 1^3 + 2^3 + 3^3 + (1 + 2 + 3)^3

252 = 2 [2^1 + 2^2 + 2^3 + 2^4 + 2^5 + 2^6]

Sum of digits of 252 = 2 + 5 + 2 = 9

252 = 9 + 18 + 27 + 36 + 45 + 54 + 63

Cube root of 16 is 2.52

If 25th Feb is written as 25/02, then

2502 can be expressed as Friedman number

$2502 = 50^2 + 2$

(Can be expressed using 2, 5, 0 and 2)

26th February

26th February can be expressed as 26/2

262 is a happy number

$4 + 36 + 4 = 44$

$16 + 16 = 32$

$9 + 4 = 13$

$1 + 9 = 10$

1

27th February

27th February can be expressed as 27/2

$272 = 17^2 - 17^1$

$272 = 2^8 + 2 * 8$

Sum of first 16 even numbers

$2 + 4 + 6 + ... + 32$

Can be expressed as sum of 4 consecutive primes

$272 = 73 + 71 + 67 + 61$

28th February

28th February can be expressed as 28/2

$282 = 2^8 + 28 - 2$

Smallest 3 digit prime sandwiched between 2 primes 281 and 283

29th February

29th February can be expressed as 29/2

The probability of being born on February 29 is therefore 97/146,097 which is ~0.07%

James Bond

March

1st March

1st March can be expressed as 1/3

$13^2 = 169 = 1 + 6 + 9 = 16 =$ square of $(1 + 3)$

$13^2 = 169 = 16 + 9 = 25 =$ square of 5

$13^2 = 169 = 16 * 9 = 144 =$ square of 12

$13^2 = 5^2 + 12^2$ (Pythagorean Triplet)

If we reverse the digits of 13 and square it, we get the reverse square of 13

$31^2 = 961$

It is the smallest prime number that can be expressed as the sum of squares of two prime numbers

$13 = 2^2 + 3^2$

$13 + (1 + 3) = 16$ which is perfect square of 4

$13 - 1 - 3 = 9$ which is perfect square of 3

$13^3 = 2197$

If we re-arrange the digits of 2197, we get 1729 which is called Ramanujan Number

1729 is the smallest number which can be expressed as sum of two cubes in two ways

$1729 = 1^3 + 12^3$

$1729 = 7^3 + 10^3$

13 is prime,

139 is prime,

1399 is prime,

13999 is prime,

139991 is prime,

1399913 is prime,

13999133 is prime

2nd March

2nd March can be expressed as 2/3

$23 = 1^2 + 2^2 + 3^2 + 3^2$

23 is a prime number

2 and 3 both are first two prime numbers

$23 = 1^4 + 2^3 + 3^2 + 4^1 + 5^0$

23! Contains 23 digits

$23! = 23 * 22 * 21 * ... * 1$

Earth is tilted at an angle of 23.44 degrees

If there are 23 people in a room, the probability of any two having same birthday is >50%

3rd March

3rd March can be expressed as 3/3

33^2 = 1089

If we reverse the 1089, we get 9801

9801 is a perfect square of 99^2

99^2 = 9801

1/33 = 3.03030303...%

$33 = 0^0 + 1^1 + 2^2 + 3^3$

$33 = 1^5 + 3^3 + 5^1$

$33 = (4 * 3 * 2 * 1) + (3 * 2 * 1) + (2 * 1) + 1 = 4! + 3! + 2! + 1!$

33 x 3367 = 111,111

333 x 333667 = 111,111,111

3333 x 33336667 = 111,111,111,111 and so on

4th March

4th March can be expressed as 4/3

$43 = 4^2 + 3^3$

$43 = 6^0 + 6^1 + 6^2$

March 4 is 64th day of a leap year (Jan-31, Feb-29 and Mar – 4)

4^3 = 64 ... 64th day of the year

43 is prime

439 is prime

4391 is prime

43913 is prime

4391339 is prime

5th March

5th March can be expressed as 5/3

$53 = 27^2 - 26^2$

$53 = 27 + 26$

$53 = 1^1 + 5^2 + 3^3$

Cube root of 149 is 5.3

$1 = 1^2$, $4 = 2^2$ and $9 = 3^2$

6th March

6th March can be expressed as 6/3

$63 = 6^2 + 3^3$

$63 = 2^0 + 2^1 + 2^2 + 2^3 + 2^4 + 2^5$

$63 = 81 - 18$

$63 = 4^{(6-3)}$

March 6 is the 65th day of the year (66th in leap years) in the Gregorian calendar

300 days remain until the end of the year

Angle between hour and minute clock at 3 minutes pas 6 is 163.5

7th March

7th March can be expressed as 7/3

73 is a star number. The nth star number is given by the formula $Sn = 6n(n - 1) + 1$

If $n = 4$, we get 73, which is the 4th Star number

73 is 1/5 of total year i.e. $73 * 5 = 365$ days

73 is a prime number

7 and 3 individually are prime too

If we reverse the digits of 73, we get 37

37 is prime too

73 is 21st prime number and 37 is 12th prime number

$73 = 37 + 36$

$73 = 37^2 - 36^2$

$73 = (7 + 3)^2 - 3^2$

$73 = 7 + 3 + (2^0 + 2^1 + 2^2 + 2^3 + 2^4 + 2^5)$

$73 = (7 - 3)^3 + 3^2$

8th March

8th March can be expressed as 8/3

$83 = 42 + 41$

$83^2 = 42^2 - 41^2$

$83 = 3^2 + 5^2 + 7^2$

$83 = 8^2 + 3^2 + 8 + 3 + 83^0$

Digits of 83 squares are in ascending order

$83^2 = 6889$

9th March

9th March can be expressed as 9/3

Birth date (9) is perfect square of birth month (3)

$93 = 9^2 + 3^2 + 9^{1/2}$

$93 = 3^1 + 3^2 + 3^4$

With just 9 straight cuts a cake can be divided into 93 pieces

$93 = 3 * 31$

3 is prime

31 is prime

331 is prime

133 is prime

10th March

10th March can be expressed as 10/3

$103 = 10^2 + 3$

103 is a prime number

Sum of birth month and birth date = 10 + 3 = 13 is also prime

$103 = (10 * 3 * 3) + (10 + 3)$

103 is a happy number

11th March

11th March can be expressed as 11/3

Both birth month (3) and birth date (11) are prime

113 is also a prime

If we reverse 113, we get 311

311 is also prime (called as emirp which is reverse of prime)

If we take last two digits of 113, we get 13

Which is also prime

If we re-arrange, 113 to get 131, which is also prime

The Major angle formed between the minute hand and hour hand at 11 past 3 is 313.5

$113 = 11^2 - 3^2 + 113^0$

12th March

12th March can be expressed as 12/3

123 Consists of first 3 natural numbers 1, 2 and 3

123 is the biggest integer which is 2 more than a perfect square and 2 less than a perfect cube

$123 = 121 + 2 = 11^2 + 2$

$123 = 125 - 2 = 5^3 - 2$

$123 = 3^4 - 3^3 - 3^2 - 3^1$

$123 = 1^0 + 2^0 + 3^0 + (1 * 2 * 3 * 4 * 5)$

13th March

13th March can be expressed as 13/3

$133 = 11^0 + 11^1 + 11^2$

$133 = 5^3 + 2^3$

$133 = (1 + 3 + 3) * 19$

The minor angle formed between the minute hand and hour hand at 13 past 3 is 13.5

4 different square consists of 5 digits: 1, 6, 7, 8 and 9

$133^2 = 17689,$

$281^2 = 78961$

$137^2 = 18769,$

$286^2 = 81796$

14th March

14th March can be expressed as 14/3

14th March is the birthday of Albert Einstein

$143 = (1 * 4 * 3)^2 - 143^0$

143 can be expressed as product of first 2 two-digit primes

$143 = 11 * 13$

143 can be expressed as sum of 3 primes

$143 = 43 + 47 + 53$

14th March written in MM/DD form, it becomes 3.14; first three digits of pi

15th March

15th March can be expressed as 15/3

$153 = 1^3 + 5^3 + 3^3$ (Armstrong Number)

$153 = 1! + 2! + 3! + 4! + 5!$

153 can be expressed using digits 1, 5 and 3

$153 = 3 * 51$ (Friedman Number)

$153 = 17 * 9$

Sum of first 17 natural numbers is 153

$17 + 16 + 15 + ... + 1$

$153 = 12^2 + 3^2$

$153 = 13^2 - 4^2$

If we add the reverse of 153 to itself we get 504,

$153 + 351 = 504$, and $504^2 = 288 \times 882$

$153 + 315 + 531 = 351 + 135 + 513$

16th March

16th March can be expressed as 16/3

$163 = 13^2 - 6$

$163 = 1 + 2 * 3^4$

163 is a prime number

If we reverse the digits of 163, we get 361

which is a perfect square of 19

17th March

17th March can be expressed as 17/3

$173 = 6^3 - 6^2 - 6^1 - 6^0$

Birth date and birth month both are prime

17 and 3 both are prime

173 is prime too

Square of 173 consists of two different digits – 2 and 9

Cube of 173 consists of three different digits – 1, 5 and 7

$173^2 = 29929$

$173^3 = 5177717$

Cube root of 3 is 1.73

If we reverse the digits of 173, we get 371

371 is third Armstrong number

$371 = 3^3 + 7^3 + 1^3$

18th March

18th March can be expressed as 18/3

$183 = 13^0 + 13^1 + 13^2$

$183 = 92 + 91$

$183 = 92^2 - 91^2$

$183 = (2^1 + 2^2 + 2^3 + 2^4 + 2^5) + (3^0 + 3^1 + 3^2 + 3^3 + 3^4)$

$428^2 = 183184$

The 183th day of the year is the midpoint of a non-leap year (because there are exactly 182 days before and 182 days after)

19th March

19th March can be expressed as 19/3

193 Each digit of 193 individually can be expressed in powers of 3

$1 = 3^0$, $9 = 3^2$ and $3 = 3^1$

193 can be expressed using digits 1, 2, 3 and 4

$193 = 14^2 - 3$

The major angle formed between the minute hand and hour hand at 3 past 19 hour is 193.5

20th March

20th March can be expressed as 20/3

$203 = 14^2 + (14/2)$

$203 = (2 * 3)^3 - 2^2 - 3^2$

203^4 consists of 4 different digits

$203^4 = 1698181681$

$203 = 1^6 + 2^5 + 3^4 + 4^3 + 5^2$

21st March

21st March can be expressed as 21/3

213 = (2 * 1 * 3)^3 − 3

213^2 = 45369 = 1! + 2! + 3! + 7! + 8!

213 = 5^3 + 4^3 + 3[2^3]

22nd March

22nd March can be expressed as 22/3

223 is a prime number

223 = 2 + 2 + 3 + (2 * 3)^3

223 = [2(2 + 2 + 3)]^2 + 3^3

223^2 = 49729

49 is a perfect square of 7

729 is a perfect square of 27

23rd March

Both birth date 23 and birth month are prime

23rd March can be expressed as 23/3

233 is also prime

2^{233} − 3 is also prime

233 = 2 + 3 + 3 + [1 + 2 + 3 + 4 + 5]^2

233 = 3^5 − 3^2 − 3^0

24th March

24th March can be expressed as 24/3

243 is the only 3 digit number which can be expressed in 5th power of an integer

243 = 3 * 3 * 3 * 3 * 3

If we add birth date and birth month, we get 27 which is 3 * 3 * 3

If we divide birth date with birth month, we get 8 which is 2 * 2 * 2

25th March

25th March can be expressed as 25/3

Sum of birth date and birth month is 25 + 3 = 28

28 is a perfect number. Factors of 28 are 1, 2, 4, 7, 14 and 28.

28 = 1 + 2 + 4 + 7 + 14

$253 = 2^7 + 2^6 + 2^5 + 2^4 + 2^3 + 2^2 + 2^1 - 2^0$

$253 = 2 * 5^3 + 3$

Sum of first 22 natural numbers is 253

253 = 1 + 2 + 3 + ... + 22

253 is a star number. The nth star number is given by the formula Sn = 6n(n − 1) + 1

If n = 7, we get 253, which is the 7th Star Number

$253^2 = 64009$

Both 64 and 009 are perfect squares of 8 and 3 respectively

If we write 25th March as 25/03, the number 2503 is a Friedman number. 2503 can be expressed using 2, 5, 0 and 3 exactly once

$2503 = 50^2 + 3$

26th March

26th March can be expressed as 26/3

$263^2 = 69169$

69169 reads the same when turned upside down (also called strobogrammatic)

263 is a prime number. If we add birth date and birth month, we get 29 which is also prime

263 can be expressed as sum of 5 primes

$263 = 43 + 47 + 53 + 59 + 61$

$263 = 2 + 6 * 3 + 3^5$

27th March

27th March can be expressed as 27/3

Absolute Zero (0 Degree Kelvin) = −273 Degree Celsius (approximate)

$273 = 2 * 7 + 3 + 2^{(7 + 1)}$

273 in base 10 = 333 in base 3

$(273)_{10} = (333)_3$

$27/3 = 9 = 3^2$

28th March

28th March can be expressed as 28/3

$283 = 2^5 + 8^1 + 3^5$

283 is prime; 83 is prime and 3 is prime

$283 = (6! - 5! - 4! - 3! - 2! - 1! - 0!)/2$

29th March

29th March can be expressed as 29/3

Both birthdate 29 and birth month 3, individually are prime

293 is also a prime

$293 = 2^8 + 9^2 + 3^4 + 3^1$

293 can be expressed as sum of 3 tetradic primes (numbers which look same when turned upside down)

$293 = 11 + 101 + 181$

30th March

30th March can be expressed as 30/3

10^{303} is called centillion. Any number higher than centillion is considered an unimaginable abstraction

303^3 = 27818127

27, 8, 1, 8, 1, 27 are cube individually

31st March

31st March can be expressed as 31/3

313 is palindrome as well as prime

313 when converted to base 2 becomes 100111001 which is also prime

$313 = 13^2 + (13 - 1)^2$

31 is prime, 13 is prime, 3 is prime

313^3 which is 9597924961 ends in 961 which is square of 31^2

April

1st April

1st April can be expressed as 1/4

$14 = 1^2 + 2^2 + 3^2$

$14 = 2^1 + 2^2 + 2^3$

$14^2 = 196$. If we rearrange 196 to make 169 it becomes 13^2 and 961 which is 31^2

$1/14 = 7.142857$

Both 1 and 4 individually are perfect square

2nd April

2nd April can be expressed as 2/4

$24 = 1 * 2 * 3 * 4$

$24 = 2^3 + 2^4$

24 has 8 factors (1, 2, 3, 4, 6, 8, 12, 24). The smallest number to have 8 factors

24 can be expressed as sum of 4 consecutive odd numbers

$24 = 3 + 5 + 7 + 9$

$24^2 = 576$. A square consists of 3 consecutive digits 5, 6 and 7.

$24^3 = 13824$ terminates in 24

Subtracting 1 from any of its divisors (except 1 and 2, but including itself) yields a prime number; 24 is the largest number with this property.

3rd April

3rd April can be expressed as 3/4

$34 = 3 + 4 + 5^2$

$3^2 + 4^2 = 5^2$ (Pythagorean Triplet)

There are 4 factors of 34 are 1, 2, 17 and 34. The neighbours of 34 are 33 and 35. Both neighbours have 4 factors.

34 is the smallest such number who has same number of factors as its neighbour

Sum of digits of 34 = 3 + 4 = 7

$34 = 7 + 8 + 9 + 10$

4th April

4th April can be expressed as 4/4

Only 12 dates have both DD equal to MM. 44 is one of them.

44 can be expressed in 4 fours = 44 + 4 − 4

$44 = 3^1 + 4^2 + 5^2$

5th April

5th April can be expressed as 5/4

54 can be written as the sum of three squares in three different ways:

$7^2 + 2^2 + 1^2 = 54$

$6^2 + 3^2 + 3^2 = 54$

$5^2 + 5^2 + 2^2 = 54$

It is the smallest number with this property

$54 = 3^3 + 3^3 = = 3^4 - 3^3$

$54 = (3^3 + 3^2 + 3^1 + 3^0) + (3^3 - 3^2 - 3^1 - 3^0)$

6th April

6th April can be expressed as 6/4

Only date which is both perfect square and perfect cube

$64 = 2^6 = 4^3 = 8^2$

Sum of first 8 odd number is 64

$64 = 1 + 3 + 5 + 7 + 9 + 11 + 13 + 15$

There are 7 divisors of 64

1, 2, 4, 8, 16, 32

It is the smallest number of have 7 divisors

$64^3 = 262, 144$

Last 3 digits are 144 which is perfect square of 12

$64^4 = 16777, 216$

Last 3 digits are 216 which is perfect cube of 6

There are 64 squares on a chess board

7th April

7th April can be expressed as 7/4

$74 = 17 + 18 + 19 + 20$

Square of 74 consists of 4 consecutive digits – 4, 5, 6 and 7

$74^2 = 5476$

$74 = 1^1 + 3^2 + 4^3$

8th April

8th April can be expressed as 8/4

$84 = 4^1 + 4^2 + 4^3$

$84 = 1 + 3 + 6 + 10 + 15 + 21 + 28$

 2 3 4 5 6 7

$84 = 2^5 + 3^3 + 5^2$

(is the smallest number that can be expressed as the sum of 3 distinct primes raised to distinct prime exponents)

9th April

9th April can be expressed as 9/4

It is 100th Day of the Calendar Year For a Leap Year (Jan – 31, Feb 29, Mar – 31, Apr – 10)

31 + 29 + 31 + 9 = 100

94 = Both 9 and 4 individually are perfect square

9 * 4 = 36 is a perfect square

9/4 = 2.25 which is again a perfect square of 1.5

If we reverse the digits of 94, we get 49 which is perfect square

$94 = 9 + 4 + 9^2$

10th April

10th April can be expressed as 10/4

It is 100th Day of the Calendar Year For a Non Leap Year (Jan – 31, Feb 28, Mar – 31, Apr – 10)

31 + 28 + 31 + 10 = 100

11th April

11th April can be expressed as 11/4

$114 = 11^2 – 11 + 4$

$114 = 3^4 + 3^3 + 3^3 – 3^1$

$114^2 = 12996$

$1 + 2 + 9 + 9 + 6 = 27 = 2 + 7 = 9$

$114^3 = 1481544$

$1 + 4 + 8 + 1 + 5 + 4 + 4 = 27 = 2 + 7 = 9$

$114^4 = 168896016$

$1 + 6 + 8 + 8 + 9 + 6 + 0 + 1 + 6 = 45 = 4 + 5 = 9$

12th April

12th April can be expressed as 12/4

Each digit of 124 individually can be expressed in 3 consecutive powers of 2

$1 = 2^0, 2 = 2^1$ and $4 = 2^2$

If we multiply all digits of $124 = 1 * 2 * 4 = 8$

124 can be expressed as sum of 8 distinct prime numbers

$5 + 7 + 11 + 13 + 17 + 19 + 23 + 29$

$124 = 12^2 - 4^2 - 4$

Both square and fourth power of 124 ends in 376

$124^2 = 15376$

$124^4 = 236421376$

13th April

13th April can be expressed as 13/4

$134 = (5 * 4 * 3 * 2) + (5 + 4 + 3 + 2)$

$134^2 - 67^2 = 13467$

If we take reciprocal of 134, the first 3 digits after decimal are 007

$1/134 = 0.007$

$134 = 11^2 + (11 + 2)$

$134 = 12^2 - (12 - 2)$

A deck of cards has 13 cards of 4 different suits

14th April

14th April can be expressed as 14/4

144 = Perfect square of 12

If we add all the digits of 144, we get 1 + 4 + 4 = 9, which is perfect square of 3

$144^2 = 20736$

If we add all the digits of 20736, we get 2 + 0 + 7 + 3 + 6 = 18 = 1 + 8 = 9

$144^3 = 2985984$

If we add all the digits of 2985084, we get 2 + 9 + 8 + 5 + 9 + 8 + 4 = 45 = 4 + 5 = 9

If we multiply all digits of 144, we get 1 * 4 * 4 = 16, which is perfect square of 4

If we write down all-natural numbers starting from 1 till 144 and add them, we get 10440

1 + 2 + 3 + ... + 144 = 10440

$144 = 12^2$

If we reverse the digits of 144, to get 441, it's perfect square of 21 (reverse digit of 12)

$441 = 21^2$

144 = (1 + 4)! + 4!

15th April

15th April can be expressed as 15/4

154 = 22 * 7

22/7 which is approximate value of Pi

154 = (5 * 4 * 3 * 2 * 1) + (4 * 3 * 2 * 1) + (3 * 2 * 1) + (2 * 1) + 1

154 = 5! + 4! + 3! + 2! + 1! + 0!

Sum of digits of 154 is 1 + 5 + 4 = 10 = 1 + 0 = 1

154^2 = 23716 = 2 + 3 + 7 + 1 + 6 = 19 = 1 + 9 = 10 = 1 + 0 = 1

154^3 = 3652264 = 3 + 6 + 5 + 2 + 2 + 6 + 4 = 28 = 2 + 8 = 10 = 1 + 0 = 1

16th April

16th April can be expressed as 16/4

Birthdate 16 is perfect square of birth month 4

164 is the smallest number which can be expressed as concatenation of two squares in two different ways

1 and 64 both are perfect squares

16 and 4 both are perfect squares

If we add the digits of 164, we get $1 + 6 + 4 = 11 = 1 + 1 = 2$

$164 = 1 * 2 * 3^4$

17th April

17th April can be expressed as 17/4

$174 = 5^2 + 6^2 + 7^2 + 8^2$

$174 = 6^3 - 6^2 - 6^1$

18th April

18th April can be expressed as 18/4

$184 = 2^3 * 23$

18th April is 108th day of the calendar year starting from 1st Jan of Non Leap Year

(Jan-31, Feb-28, Mar-31, Apr-18)

There are 256 more days remaining in the calendar year

$256 = 2^8 = 4^4 = 16^2$

184 consists of 1, 8 and 4 which can be expressed in first 3 powers of 2

$1 = 2^0$, $8 = 2^3$ and $4 = 2^2$

19th April

19th April can be expressed as 19/4

194 consists of 1, 9 and 4. Each digit itself is a perfect square

$1 = 1^2$, $9 = 3^2$ and $4 = 2^2$

194 is sum of squares of three consecutive squares

$194 = 7^2 + 8^2 + 9^2$

Sum of digits of $194 = 1 + 9 + 4 = 14$

$194 = 14^2 - 2$

Smallest number that can be written as the sum of 3 squares in 5 ways

20th April

20th April can be expressed as 20/4

$204 = 1^2 + 2^2 + 3^2 + ... + 8^2$

$204 = 20 + 19 + 18 + ... + 4$

$204^2 = 23^3 + 24^3 + 25^3$

$204^2 = 41616$

21st April

21st April can be expressed as 21/4

$214 = 2^3 + 3^3 + 3^3 + 33 + 5^3$

214 consists of 2, 1 and 4. Each can be expressed in powers of 2

$2 = 2^1$, $1 = 2^0$ and $4 = 2^2$

21st April is 111th day of the calendar for a non-leap year (Jan-31, Feb -28, Mar – 31 and April – 21)

$31 + 28 + 31 + 21 = 111$

22nd April

22nd April can be expressed as 22/4

$224 = 2 * 112$

22nd April is 112th day of the calendar for a non-leap year (Jan-31, Feb -28, Mar – 31 and April – 22)

$31 + 28 + 31 + 21 = 112$

$224 = 4^4 – 3^3 – 2^2 – 1^1$

$224 = 4 * 56$ (Consisting of 4, 5 and 6)

$224 = 2^3 + 3^3 + 4^3 + 5^3$

$224 = [2(2 + 2 + 4)]^2 – [2(2 * 2 * 4)]$

23rd April

23rd April can be expressed as 23/4

234 consist of 3 consecutive digits 2, 3 and 4. Only 5 such dates are possible

$234 = 2[2 + 3 + 4]^2 – [2 + 3 + 4]$

$234^2 = 54756$

Square of 234 consists of 4 digits 4, 5, 6 and 7

If we write 23rd April as 23/04, then 2304 is perfect square of 48

24th April

24th April can be expressed as 24/4

$244 = 2^{(4 + 4)} - 2 - 2 - 4 - 4$

$244 = 3^5 + 1^5$

Smallest number (after 2) which can be expressed as sum of 5th power of 2 numbers

$244^3 = 14526784$

Cube of 244 ends in 784 which is a perfect square of 27

If 25th April is written as 25/04, then

2504 can be expressed as Friedman number

$2504 = 50^2 + 4$

(Can be expressed using 2, 5, 0 and 4)

25th April

25th April can be expressed as 25/4

Both birthdate and birth month are perfect square. 25 is perfect square of 5 and 4 is perfect square of 2

$25/4 = 6.25$

6.25 is a perfect square of 2.5

$254 = 2^8 - 2$

$254^3 = 4162314256$

Cube of 254 ends in 256

254 can be expressed using 2, 3, 4 and 5

$254 = 2 * 5^3 + 4$

26th April

26th April can be expressed as 26/4

$264 = 2 * 66 * 4$

$264 = 2^5 + 6^3 + 4^2$

$264 = (2 + 6 + 4)^2 + (1 * 2 * 3 * 4 * 5)$

We get six 2 digits number which can be formed from 264. If we add them, we get 264

$26 + 62 + 24 + 42 + 64 + 46 = 264$

$264^2 = 69696$

Square of 264 consists of only 2 digits 6 and 9. It is palindrome and undulating

27th April

27th April can be expressed as 27/4

$274 = 2^0 + 2^1 + 2^2 + 2^3 + 2^4 + 3^5$

$274 = 16^2 + 16 + 2$

$274^2 = 75076$

If we write all-natural numbers starting from 1 to 274 and add them, we get 37675

Cube of 274 ends in 276

$274^3 = 5636405776$

If we write 27th April as 27/04, we get 2704 which is a perfect square of 52

28th April

28th April can be expressed as 28/4

284 Each digit individually can be expressed in power of 2

$2 = 2^1$, $4 = 2^2$ and $8 = 2^3$

$284 = 28 + 4^4$

The 5 divisors of 284 (excluding itself) are 1, 2, 4, 71 and 142

If we add them, we get 220

The factors of 220 (excluding 120) are 1, 2, 4, 5, 10, 11, 20, 22, 44, 55, 110

And if we add them, we get 284. Hence, 220 and 284 are amicable

It is the smallest such pair and the only possible pair below 1000

29th April

29th April can be expressed as 29/4

$11115^2 - 294^2 = 123,456,789$

$294 = 2^1 + 3^2 + 3^3 + 4^4$

30th April

30th April can be expressed as 30/4

$304 = 3^5 + 0 + 4^3 - 3$

304 is the sum of six consecutive primes

$304 = 41 + 43 + 47 + 53 + 59 + 61$

Also sum of eight consecutive primes

$304 = 23 + 29 + 31 + 37 + 41 + 43 + 47 + 53$

May

1ˢᵗ May

1ˢᵗ May can be expressed as 1/5

If we add all digits starting from 1 and ending in 5, we get 15

$15 = 1 + 2 + 3 + 4 + 5$

$15 = (5 - 1)^2 - 1^2$

There are 15 balls in a snooker triangle

The only 15-letter word that can be spelled without repeating a letter is "uncopyrightable"

15 is the product of first two odd prime numbers

$15 = 3 * 5$

$15^2 = 225$

If we add all digits of 225 = 2 + 2 + 5 we get 9, which is a perfect square of 3

2ⁿᵈ May

2ⁿᵈ May can be expressed as 2/5

25 can be expressed using digits 2 and 5 (Only such 2 digit number exists). Such numbers are called Friedman number

$25 = 5^2$

25 is the smallest square which can be expressed as sum of two squares

9 + 16 = 25

$3^2 + 4^2 = 5^2$

$25^2 = 625$

$25^3 = 15625$

$25^4 = 390625$

$25^5 = 9765625$

$25^6 = 244140625$ and so on

25 and 76 are only two 2 digits number whose square end in the same digits as the number itself

$25^2 = 625$

$76^2 = 5776$

Sum of First 5 Odd Numbers is 25

1 + 3 + 5 + 7 + 9 = 25

3rd May

3rd May can be expressed as 3/5

35 consist of First 2 Odd Prime Numbers 3 and 5

35 = (10 − 3) * * (10 − 5)

35 = 1 + 3 + 6 + 10 + 15

    2   3   4   5

35 = 5^2 + (5 * 2)

4th May

4th May can be expressed as 4/5

$45^2 = 2025$

$45 = 20 + 25$

(45 is first such number called as Kaprekar number)

45 is sum of first 9 natural numbers

$45 = 1 + 2 + 3 + 4 + 5 + 6 + 7 + 8 + 9$

$45^3 = 91125$

$45 = 9 + 11 + 25$

$45^4 = 4100625$

$45 = 4 + 10 + 06 + 25$

If we reverse 45, we get 54

$45 = 54 - 5 - 4$

1/45 is 2.2222...%

5th May

5th May can be expressed as 5/5

5th May is 125 day of non-leap calendar year (Jan-31, Feb-28, Mar-31, Apr-30, May-5)

$125 = 31 + 28 + 31 + 30 + 5$

125 is the perfect cube of 5

$55^2 = 3025$

55 = 30 + **25**

(Kaprekar Number)

1/55 = 1.81818181...%

Sum of first 10 natural number is 55

55 = 1 + 2 + 3 + 4 + 5 + 6 + 7 + 8 + 9 + 10

$55 = 5^2 + 5^2 + 5$

Sum of square of first 5 digits is 55

$55 = 5^2 + 4^2 + 3^2 + 2^2 + 1^2$

55 can be expressed in power of 2's and 3's

$55 = 2^0 + 2^1 + 2^2 + 2^3 + 3^0 + 3^1 + 3^2 + 3^3$

55 can be expressed in square form of first 10 natural numbers

$55 = 10^2 - 9^2 + 8^2 - 7^2 + 6^2 - 5^2 + 4^2 - 3^2 + 2^2 - 1^2$

$3^2 + 4^2 = 5^2$

$33^2 + 44^2 = 55^2$

6th May

6th May can be expressed as 6/5

65 can be expressed using first 3 odd numbers

65 = 13 * 5

65 can be expressed using numbers 1 to 5 with powers consisting from 1 to 5

$65 = 5^1 + 4^2 + 3^3 + 2^4 + 1^5$

Sum of digits of 65 = 6 + 5 = 11

65 + 56 = 121 which is perfect square of 11

65 − 56 = 9 which is perfect square of 3

65 is the smallest number that becomes square if its reverse is either added or subtracted from it

65 is the smallest integer that can be expressed as a sum of two distinct positive squares in two ways,

$65 = 8^2 + 1^2$

$65 = 7^2 + 4^2$

7th May

7th May can be expressed as 7/5

If we start adding the digits of 75 and keep adding the previous number we get 75

7 + 5 = 12

5 + 12 = 17

12 + 17 = 29

17 + 29 = 46

29 + 46 = 75

$75 = 7^2 + 5^2 + 1$

If we reverse 75, we get 57

Square-root of 75 is approximately 5.7

8th May

$85 = 4^3 + 4^2 + 4^1 + 4^0$

The smallest number that can be expressed as a sum of two squares, with all squares greater than 1, in two ways,

$85 = 9^2 + 2^2$

$85 = 7^2 + 6^2$

9th May

9th May can be expressed as 9/5

$95 = 9 + 5 + 9^2$

Square of 95 starts with 9 and ends with 5

$95^2 = 9025$

Smallest such 4-digit square

10th May

10th May can be expressed as 10/5

$105 = 3 * 5 * 7$ (product of first 3 odd primes)

$105 = (1 * 2 * 3 * 4 * 5) - (1 + 2 + 3 + 4 + 5)$

The largest number n known such that $n - 2k$ is prime for k = >1 (Erdös conjecture)

$105 - 2^1 = 103$; (103 is prime)

$105 - 2^2 = 101$; (101 is prime)

$105 - 2^3 = 97$; (97 is prime)

$105 - 2^4 = 89$; (89 is prime)

$105 - 2^5 = 73$; (73 is prime)

$105 - 2^6 = 41$ (41 is prime)

105 is sum of first 14 natural numbers

$105 = 1 + 2 + 3 + ... + 14$

$105^2 = 11025$

11th May

11th May can be expressed as 11/5

$115 = 5! - 5$

$115^2 = 13225$

225 is perfect square of 15

$115 = 23 * (2 + 3)$

Both 11 and 5 are prime numbers

Sum of all digits of $115 = 1 + 1 + 5 = 7$ is also prime

Product of all digits of $1 * 1 * 5 = 5$ is also prime

12th May

12th May can be expressed as 12/5

$125 = 5^{(1 + 2)}$

Smallest three-digit Friedman Number; can be expressed using the digits of the number i.e. 125 can be expressed using 1, 2 and 5

$125^2 = 15625$

25 is a perfect square

625 is also a perfect square

5625 is also a perfect square

$125 = (1 * 2 * 3 * 4 * 5) + 5$

$125 = 2^6 + 2^5 + 2^4 + 2^3 + 2^2 + 2^1 - 2^0$

$125 = (1 * 2 * 5)^2 + 5^2$

If we reverse 125, we get 521

$521 = 5^4 - 5^3 + 5^2 - 5^1 + 5^0$

13th May

13th May can be expressed as 13/5

135 consist of first 3 odd numbers

$135 = 1^1 + 3^2 + 5^3$

$135 = (1 * 3 * 5)(1 + 3 + 5)$

$1/135 = 0.007$

14th May

14th May can be expressed as 14/5

$145 = 1! + 4! + 5! = 1 + 24 + 120$

The only factorion possible for a 3-digit number

$145 = 3^4 + 4^3 = 81 + 64$

$145 = (1 * 4 * 5) + 5^{(4 - 1)}$

Sum of digits of 145 = 1 + 4 + 5 = 10 = 1 + 0 = 1

$145^2 = 21025$

If we add the digits 21025 = 2 + 1 + 0 + 2 + 5 = 10 = 1 + 0 = 1

$145^3 = 3048625 = 3 + 0 + 4 + 8 + 6 + 2 + 5 = 28 = 2 + 8 = 10 = 1 + 0 = 1$

15th May

15th May can be expressed as 15/5

$155 = 5^1 + 5^2 + 5^3$

$155 = 5 * 31$

If we list all prime number between 5 and 31, we get

5, 7, 11, 13, 17, 19, 23 and 27

7 + 11 + 13 + 17 + 19 + 23 + 29 + 31 = 155

16th May

16th May can be expressed as 16/5

If we add all digits of 165 = 1 + 6 + 5, we get 12

$165 = 12^2 + 21^1$

$165^2 = 27225$

25 is a perfect square of 5

225 is a perfect square of 15

7225 is a perfect square of 85

17th May

17th May can be expressed as 17/5

$175 = 1^1 + 7^2 + 5^3$

$175 = 1 * 7 * 5^2$

18th May

18th May can be expressed as 18/5

Square of 185 consists of consecutive digits 2, 3, 4 and 5

$185^2 = 34225$

25 is a perfect square of 5

225 is a perfect square of 15

4225 is a perfect square of 65

$1/185 = 0.0054054054054...$

19th May

19th May can be expressed as 19/5

$205 = 4^4 - 4^3 + 4^2 - 4^1$

$195 = (1 + 9 + 5)^2 - 2 * (1 + 9 + 5)$

$195 = (9 + 5)^2 - 1^2$

Both birthdate – 19 and birth month – 5 are prime numbers

191, 193, 195 and 197 are prime numbers. If we take average of above 4 prime numbers, we get 195

20th May

20th May can be expressed as 20/5

$205 = 4^4 - 4^3 + 4^2 - 4^1 + 4^0$

$205 = (20)^2/2 + 5$

Square of 205 contains 205

$205^2 = 42025$

25 is a perfect square of 5

2025 is a perfect square of 45

$205 = 5 * 41$

If we convert 205 of decimal system to base 6, we get 541

$(205)_{10} = (541)_6$

$205 = 2^3 + 3^3 + 4^3 + 2^3$

21st May

21st May can be expressed as 21/5

$215 = (2 + 1 + 5)^3 - 1$

$215 = [(2 + 1) * 5]^2 - (2 * 1 * 5)$

If we reverse the digits of 215, we get 512

$512 = (5 + 1 + 2)^3$

21st May is 142 day of a leap year (Jan-31, Feb-29, Mar-31, Apr-30 and May – 21). 225 days remain until the end of the year

225 is the perfect square of 15 which is the last two digits of 215

The Cube of 10 (2 * 1 * 5) is 2.15

22nd May

22nd May can be expressed as 22/5

225 is a perfect square of 15

$225 = (1 + 2 + 3 + 4 + 5)^2$

$225 = 1^3 + 2^3 + 3^3 + 4^3 + 5^3$

225 can be expressed as product of two perfect squares

$225 = 3^2 * 5^2$

$225 = 113 + 112$

$225 = 113^2 – 112^2$

$225 = 4^4 – 3^3 – 2^2$

23rd May

23rd May can be expressed as 23/5

$235 = (2 + 3 + 5) + (1 + 2 + 3 + 4 + 5)^2$

$235 = (2 + 3 + 5) + (1^3 + 2^3 + 3^3 + 4^3 + 5^3)$

Square of 235 consists of two 2's and three 5's

$235^2 = 55225$

May 23 is the 143rd day of the year (144th in leap years) in the Gregorian calendar

222 days remain until the end of the year

24th May

24th May can be expressed as 24/5

$245 = 49 * (9 - 5)$

$245 = 8^2 + 9^2 + 10^2$

$245 = (1 * 2 * 3 * 4 * 5) + (5 * 5 * 5)$

$(245)_{10} = (365)_8$

365 is the number of days in a non-leap year

25th May

25th May can be expressed as 25/5

$255 = 2^8 - 1$

$255 = 2^{2^3} - 1$

$255 = 2 * (5^3) + 5$

$255 = 4^4 - 1$

$255 = 17^2 - (17 * 2)$

255 in base 10 = 11111111 in base 2

$(255)_{10} = (11111111)_2$

If 25th May is written as 25/05, then

2505 can be expressed as Friedman number

$2505 = 50^2 + 5$

(Can be expressed using 2, 5, 0 and 5)

26th May

26th May can be expressed as 26/5

$265 = 11^2 + 12^2$

$265^2 = 264^2 + 23^2$

Cube of 265 ends in 625

$265^3 = 18609625$

Square of 7 is 2.65

27th May

27th May can be expressed as 27/5

$275 = (2 + 7 + 5)^2 + (2 * 7 * 5) + (2 + 7)$

$275^2 = 75625$

25 is a perfect square of 5

625 is a perfect square of 25

5625 is a perfect square of 75

75625 is a perfect square of 275

28th May

28th May can be expressed as 28/5

Sum of Square of all single digit numbers

$285 = 9^2 + 8^2 + 7^2 + ... + 1^2$

$285^2 = 81225$

25 is a perfect square of 5

225 is a perfect square of 15

1225 is a perfect square of 35

81225 is a perfect square of 285

$285 = (2 + 8 + 5) * [(28 + 5 + 5)/2]$

29th May

29th May can be expressed as 29/5

$(2 + 9 + 5)^3 = 216$

216 days remain until the end of the year.

May 29 is the 149th day of the year (150th in leap years) in the Gregorian calendar

$1 = 1^2, 4 = 2^2$ and $9 = 3^2$

Birth date – 29 and birth month -5, both are prime

295 is product of two primes 59 * 5

2 * 295 + 9 * 295 + 5 * 295 + 1 is also prime

30th May

30th May can be expressed as 30/5

$305^2 = 93025$

25 is a perfect square of 5

3025 is a perfect square of 55

93025 is a perfect square of 305

May 30 is the 150th day of the year (151st in leap years) in the Gregorian calendar

$305 = (30 * 5) + (30 * 5) + 5$

31st May

31st May can be expressed as 31/5

$315 = 3^2 * 5 * 7$

$315 = (10 - 3) * (10 - 1) * (10 - 5)$

$315 = (4 + 3) * (4 + 1) * (4 + 5)$

$3^2 = 9$ and $15^2 = 225$

$315^2 = 99225$

Both 31 and 5 are prime numbers

If we re-arrange 315, to get 153 which is

$153 = 1^3 + 5^3 + 3^3$

$513 = (5 + 3)^3 + 1$

June

1st June

1st June can be expressed as 1/6

16 is the only integer of the form $x^y = y^x$ (where, x is not equal to y)

$16 = 4^2 = 2^4$

Sum of first 4 odd numbers

$16 = 1 + 3 + 5 + 7$

The smallest number which is the sum of two distinct primes in two ways,

$16 = 3 + 13$

$16 = 5 + 11$

Also, if we reverse the number, we get 61 which is also a prime

2nd June

2nd June can be expressed as 2/6

26 is the only number sandwiched between a perfect square ($5^2 = 25$) and a perfect cube ($3^3 = 27$)

$26 = 1^2 + 4^2 + 3^2$

26 can be expressed using digits 1, 2 and 3

$26 = 2 * 13$

$26^2 = 676$

The smallest non-palindrome whose square is palindrome

$26^3 = 17576$

If we add the digits of $17576 = 1 + 7 + 5 + 7 + 6 = 26$

26 is the number of the alphabets

3rd June

3rd June can be expressed as 3/6

$36 = 1^3 + 2^3 + 3^3$

$36 = (1 + 2 + 3)^2$

$36 = (3 + 6) * 4$

36 is largest 2-digit number which is divisible by product of its digits (3 * 6) and sum of its digits (3 + 6)

Sum of first 36 natural numbers is 666

$36 + 35 + 34 + ... + 1 = 666$

If we toss two die, there are 36 possible outcomes

1361 is prime

136361 is prime

13636361 is prime

1363636361 is prime

Cube of 36 consists of only 3 consecutive digits 4, 5 and 6. Also the cube contains three 6's

$36^3 = 46656$

4th June

4th June can be expressed as 4/6

$46 = 4 + 6 + 6^2$

$46 = 1^1 + 2^1 + 3^3 + 4^2$

The sum of digits of 46 is equal to the sum of digit of its square

$46 = 4 + 6 = 10$

$46^2 = 2116$

$2116 = 2 + 1 + 1 + 6 = 10$

Reverse of 46, gives 64

$64 = 2^6 = 4^3 = 8^2$

46^4 ends in 456

$46^4 = 4477456$

Homo-sapiens have 46 chromosomes in every cell

5th June

5th June can be expressed as 5/6

$56 = 7 * 8$

Forms a series 5, 6, 7 and 8

$56 = 7^2 + 7$

$56 = 8^2 - 8$

$(111 + 1)/(1 + 1) = 56$

$(222 + 2)/(2 + 2) = 56$

$(333 + 3)/(3 + 3) = 56$

...

$(999 + 9)/(9 + 9) = 56$

$56 = 1 + 3 + 6 + 10 + 15 + 21$

$\qquad$ 2 $\quad$ 3 $\quad$ 4 $\quad$ 5 $\quad$ 6

June 5 is 156th day of a non-leap year (Jan – 31, Feb – 28, Mar – 31, Apr – 30, May 31 and Jun – 5)

6th June

6th June can be expressed as 6/6

Square of 66 consists of 4 consecutive digits 3, 4, 5 and 6

$66^2 = 4356$

$66 = 11 * 6$

Sum of first 11 natural numbers is 66

$66 = 11 + 10 + 9 + ... + 1$

Square of 44 is approximately 6.6

$1/66 = 1.51515151...\%$

$66 = 2^6 + 2$

If we take sum of all divisors of 66, we get a perfect square

$1 + 2 + 3 + 6 + 11 + 22 + 33 + 66 = 144 = 12^2$

7th June

7th June can be expressed as 7/6

$76 = 2^6 + 2 * 6$

$76 = 4^3 + 4 * 3$

Last 2 digit on any power of 76 ends in 76 (automorphic number). Largest such 2-digit number

$76^2 = 5776$

$76^3 = 438976$

$76^4 = 33362176$

8th June

8th June can be expressed as 8/6

$86 = 3^2 + 4^2 + 5^2 + 6^2$

$86 = 43 * 2$

(consists of consecutive digits 4, 3 and 2)

$86 = 8^2 + 6^2 - (8 + 6)$

Cube root of 86 is 4.41 which is square of 2.1

9th Jun

9th June can be expressed as 9/6

$96 = 9 + 6 + 9^2$

96 when read upside down becomes 96

Smallest number that can be expressed as the difference of 2 squares in 4 different ways

$96 = 25^2 - 23^2$

$96 = 14^2 - 10^2$

$96 = 11^2 - 5^2$

$96 = 10^2 - 2^2$

Product of digits gives 54 (9 * 6)

$96 = 5! - 4! = (1 * 2 * 3 * 4 * 5) - (1 * 2 * 3 * 4)$

Square of 96 starts with 9 and ends with 6

$96^2 = 9216$

Largest such two-digit number

10th June

10th June can be expressed as 10/6

Square of 106 contains 123 in the middle

$106^2 = 11236$

$106 = 9^2 + 5^2$

$106 = 2(2^2) + 2(7^2)$

$106 = 25 + 26 + 27 + 28$

11ᵗʰ June

11ᵗʰ June can be expressed as 11/6

Square of 116 consists of digits in ascending order

$116^2 = 13456$

$116 = 11^2 - 11 + 6$

$116 = (11 * 6) + (11 * 6) - 16$

$116 = 5^3 - 3^2$

$116 = 10^2 + 4^2$

12ᵗʰ June

12ᵗʰ June can be expressed as 12/6

$126 = 2^1 + 2^2 + 2^3 + 2^4 + 2^5 + 2^6$

$126 = 4^2 + 5^2 + 6^2 + 7^2$

If we reverse the digits of 126, we get 621

$126 = 6 * 21$

If we re-arrange the digits of 126, we get $216 = 6^3$

Cube root of 2 is approximately 1.26

13ᵗʰ June

13ᵗʰ June can be expressed as 13/6

$136 = 2^3 + 4^3 + 4^3$

$1^3 + 3^3 + 6^3 = 244$

1 and 36 both are perfect square of 1 and 6 respectively

Sum of first 16 natural numbers is 136

$1 + 2 + 3 + ... + 16 = 136$

14th June

14th June can be expressed as 14/6

$146 = (1 + 4 + 6)^2 + (1 * 4 * 6) + 146^0$

Square and cube of 146 share the same digits – 1, 2, 3 and 6

$146^2 = 21316$

$146^3 = 3112136$

June 14 is the 165th day of the year (166th in leap years) in the Gregorian calendar

Exact 200 days remain until the end of the year

15th June

15th June can be expressed as 15/6

The sum of digits of 156 = 1 + 5 + 6 = 12

$156 = 12^2 + 12$

$156 = 13^2 – 13$

The following equation contains all digits from 1 to 9 once

$156 = 2 * 78 = 39 * 4$

156 can be expressed in $x^3 + x^2 + x^1 + x^0$

$156 = 5^3 + 5^2 + 5^1 + 5^0$

The hands of clock strike 156 times in a day

Clock strikes once at 1, twice at 2, thrice at 3 and so on. But it only strikes 12 times once

No. Of times clock strikes =

$2 \times (1 + 2 + 3 + 4 + 5 + 6 + 7 + 8 + 9 + 10 + 11 + 12)$

$= 78 \times 2$

$= 156$ times

16th June

16th June can be expressed as 16/6

$166 = (1 + 6 + 6)^2 - 1^0 - 6^0 - 6^0$

Sum of digits of 166 = 1 + 6 + 6 = 13 is a prime number

166 when reversed becomes 661, which is a prime number

If 661 is turned upside down it becomes 199, which is a prime number

166 when turned upside down becomes 991, which is a prime number

166! -1 is also a prime

17th June

17th June can be expressed as 17/6

All power of 176 ends in 76

$176^2 = 30976$

$176^3 = 5451776$

$173^4 = 959512576$

18th June

18th June can be expressed as 18/6

$186 = 4 * (1 * 8 * 6) - 4$

$186 = 6^{(18/6)} - (1 + 8 + 6) - (1 + 8 + 6)$

$18^2 = 324$

$6^2 = 36$

Sum of 324 and 36 = 360 which makes a complete circle

19th June

19th June can be expressed as 19/6

$196 = 14^2$

196 is product of two perfect squares

$196 = 4 * 49 = 2^2 * 7^2$

If we re-arrange 196, we get 169

$169 = 13^2$

If we reverse the digits of 169, we get $961 = 31^2$ which is reverse of 13

Sum of first 14 odd number is 196

$1 + 3 + 5 + \ldots + 27 = 196$

196 days remain until the end of the year including 19th Jun

$196 = 365 - 31 - 28 - 31 - 30 - 18$

June 19 is the 170th day of the year (171st in leap years) in the Gregorian calendar. (Jan – 31, Feb – 28, Mar – 31, Apr – 30, Jun – 19)

20th June

20th June can be expressed as 20/6

206 = Two Hundred and Six

206 is the smallest number when written in words contains all vowels: a, e, i, o and u

$206 = 1^3 + 2^3 + 3^3 + 4^3 + 5^3$

There are 206 bones in the typical adult human body

The major angle between minute hand and hour hand at 6 minutes past 20 hours is 207

21st June

21st June can be expressed as 21/6

216 is the smallest cube which is sum of three cubes

$216 = 3^3 + 4^3 + 5^3$

216 is a Friedman number; can be expressed using 2, 1 and 6

$216 = 6^{(2 + 1)} = 6^3$

If we add all numbers starting from 21 to 6, we get 216

$21 + 20 + 19 + ... + 6 = 216$

Cube of 216 consists of only 3 consecutive digits: 4, 5 and 6

$216^2 = 46656$

22nd June

22nd June can be expressed as 22/6

If we raise 226 to the power of pi, the first 3 digits are 226

Pi^226 = 226...

$226 = 15^2 + 1$

$226 = 2 + 2 + 6 + 6 * 6 * 6$

All powers greater than 2 of 226 ends in 76

$226^2 = 51076$

$226^3 = 11543176$

$226^4 = 2608757776$

23rd June

23rd June can be expressed as 23/6

The product of digits of the date (2 * 3) gives the month – 6

236 = 2 * 2 * 59

2 + 2 + 59 = 63 which is reverse of 36

36 = 2 * 3 * 6

Cube of 236 consists of 1, 2, 3, 4 and 5

236^3 = 13144256

24th June

24th June can be expressed as 24/6

246 = (3 * 3 * 3 * 3 * 3) + 3

246 = 123 * 2

246 = (2^2^3) – 4 – 6

The digits are in progression: 2, 4 and 6 with a difference of 2

246 = $_9C_2$ + $_9C_4$ + $_9C_6$

25th June

25th June can be expressed as 25/6

256 = 2^8 = 4^4 = 16^2

256 = 2 * 5^3 + 6

$256 = 3^0 + 3^1 + 3^2 + 3^5$

Square root of $256 = 16 = 2 * 5 + 6$

$256 = 2 + 5 + 6 + 3^5$

26th June

26th June can be expressed as 26/6

$266 = 2 + 6 + 6 + 6^2 + 6^3$

$266 = 2^8 + 2 + 8$

The average gestation period of human beings is around 38 weeks or 266 days

27th June

27th June can be expressed as 27/6

276 can be expressed as 5th power of 1, 2 and 3

$276 = 1^5 + 2^5 + 3^5$

$276 = 2^3 * 3 * 23$

$276^2 = 76176$

$276^3 = 21024576$

$276^4 = 5802782976$

Sum of first 23 natural number is 276

$1 + 2 + 3 + ... + 23$

28th June

28th June can be expressed as 28/6

Sum of digits of 286 = 2 + 8 + 6 = 16 which is a perfect square of 4

Difference of birth date and birth month is 22

22^2 = 484 which is palindrome (reads same backwards)

Square root of 286 is 16.91

1691 when turn upside down remains 1691

4 different square consists of 5 digits: 1, 6, 7, 8 and 9

286^2 = 81796

137^2 = 18769,

133^2 = 17689,

281^2 = 78961

29th June

29th June can be expressed as 29/6

$296 = 2^3 + 2^5 + 2^8$

Cube of 296 is 6.66

30 June

30th June can be expressed as 30/6

$306 = 17^2 + 17 = 289 + 17$

$306 = 18^2 - 18 = 324 - 18$

Square of 306 ends with 3636

$306^2 = 93636$

July

1st July

1st July can be expressed as 1/7

$17 = 2^3 + 3^2$

$17 = 3^4 - 4^3$

Smallest number that can be expressed as sum of a cube and a square in two ways

$17 = 2^3 + 3^2$

$17 = 1^3 + 4^2$

$17^3 = 4913$

Sum of digits of $4913 = 4 + 9 + 1 + 3 = 17$

$4913 = (4 + 9 + 1 + 3)^3$

$17^2 = 289$

$17^2 = 0^0 + 1^1 + 2^2 + 3^3 + 4^4$

2nd July

2nd July can be expressed as 2/7

The midpoint of the calendar year as there are 182 days before and 182 days after 2nd July

$27 = (2 + 7)^3 = 3^3$

Sum of digits of $27 = 2 + 7 = 9$ which is a perfect square of 3

$3^3 = 27$

27 is the largest number that is the sum of the digits of the cube

$27^3 = 19,883$

$1 + 9 + 8 + 8 + 3 = 27$

If we add the digits starting from 2 till 7 we get 27

$2 + 3 + 4 + 5 + 6 + 7 = 27$

The following equation contains each digit from 1 to 9; each used exactly once

$27 * 198 = 5346$

$27 = 14 + 13$

$27 = 14^2 - 13^2$

$1/37 = 0.027027027...$, and $1/27 = 0.037037037...$ (This is related to the fact that 37 x 27 = 999)

3rd July

3rd July can be expressed as 3/7

37 is a prime number

3 and 7 both are individually prime too

If we reverse 37, we get 73, which is prime too

On a calculator, any row, column or diagonal typed forwards and then backwards is divisible by 37. For example:

147741 divided by 37 = 3993

852258 divided by 37 = 23034

753357 divided by 37 = 20361

A 6-digit number in which the first 3 digits are consecutively increasing numbers; and the last 3 digits, consecutively decreasing numbers, is divisible by 37

For instance, the numbers 123987, 234765 and 567543 are all divisible by 37

3 x 37 = 111 and 1 + 1 + 1 = 3

6 x 37 = 222 and 2 + 2 + 2 = 6

9 x 37 = 333 and 3 + 3 + 3 = 9

12 x 37 = 444 and 4 + 4 + 4 = 12

15 x 37 = 555 and 5 + 5 + 5 = 15

18 x 37 = 666 and 6 + 6 + 6 = 18

21 x 37 = 777 and 7 + 7 + 7 = 21

24 x 37 = 888 and 8 + 8 + 8 = 24

27 x 37 = 999 and 9 + 9 + 9 = 27

'Normal' human body temperature is approximately 37 degrees Celsius

1/37 = 0.027027027..., and 1/27 = 0.037037037... (This is related to the fact that 37 x 27 = 999)

37 is a star number. The nth star number is given by the formula $S_n = 6n(n - 1) + 1$

If n = 3, we get 37, which is the 3th Star Number

4th July

4th July can be expressed as 4/7

47 is a prime number

47 = 24 + 23

$47 = 24^2 - 23^2$

$4^3 + 7^3 = 407$

$47 = 2^2 + 5^2 - 2 * 5$

5th July

5th July can be expressed as 5/7

$57 = 7^0 + 7^1 + 7^2$

$57 = 2^5 + 5^2 = 32 + 25$

57 = 29 + 28

$57 = 29^2 - 28^2$

Each 5 and 7 are prime numbers

6th July

6th July can be expressed as 6/7

67 is a prime number

67 = 34 + 33

$67 = 34^2 - 33^2$

A pizza can be cut into 67 slides by making just a dozen cuts

7th July

7th July can be expressed as 7/7

$77 = 4^2 + 5^2 + 6^2$

$77 = 39 + 38$

$77 = 39^2 - 38^2$

Cube of 77 consists of 4 consecutive digits – 3, 4, 5 and 6

$77^3 = 456533$

77 is product of two consecutive primes 7 and 11

$77 = 7 * 11$

Can be expressed as sum of the first 8 prime numbers

$77 = 2 + 3 + 5 + 7 + 11 + 13 + 17 + 19$

$77 = 7^2 + 7 * 2^2$

8th July

8th July can be expressed as 8/7

2, 3, 5 and 7 are first 4 prime numbers. If we take a square of them and add, we get 87

$87 = 2^2 + 3^2 + 5^2 + 7^2$

$87 = 44 + 43$

$87 = 44^2 - 43^2$

9th July

9th July can be expressed as 9/7

Sum of digits of 97 = 9 + 7 = 16 is a perfect square of 4

$97 = 9^2 + 9 + 7$

97 is 25th prime number; largest 2 digit prime number and if we reverse it's digit to get 79, we get prime too

97 = prime

907 = prime

9007 = prime

90007 = prime

900007 = prime

Smallest number with the property that its first 3 multiples contain the digit 9

97 * 1 = 97

97 * 2 = 194

97 * 3 = 291

97 = 49 + 48

$97 = 49^2 - 48^2$

$97 = 2^4 + 3^4$

$97^2 = 9409$

Each digit of 9409 is a perfect square individually: 9, 4, 0 and 9

10th July

10th July can be expressed as 10/7

$107 = 1 + 0 + 7 + 2^3 + 3^3 + 4^3$

$107^2 = 11449$

1, 4 and 9 are perfect square of 1, 2 and 3

$107^3 = 1225043$

First 4 digits – 1225 is perfect square of 35

11th July

11th July can be expressed as 11/7

7 and 11 are consecutive prime

$117 = (1 + 1 + 7) * 13 = 9 * 13$

$117 = (1 + 1)^7 - 11 = 2^7 - 11$

$117 = (7 - 1 - 1)^3 - (1 + 1)^3 = 5^3 - 2^3$

12th July

12th July can be expressed as 12/7

127 is a Friedman number; can be expressed using digits 1, 2 and 7

$127 = 2^7 - 1$

$127 = 2^0 + 2^1 + 2^2 + 2^3 + 2^4 + 2^5 + 2^6$

$127 = 5^3 + 2$

$127 = 5 * 4 * 3 * 2 * 1 + 5$

127 is a prime and if we re-arrange the digits of get 271; is also prime

127 is the smallest number which can be expressed sum of first 2 or more odd primes

$127 = 3 + 5 + 7 + 11 + 13 + 17 + 19 + 23 + 29$

$127^2 = 16129$

If we reverse last 4 digits of 16129, we get 9216

9216 is perfect square of 96

13th July

13th July can be expressed as 13/7

Both 13 and 7 are prime

3 is prime, 7 is prime, 13 is prime , 37 is prime and 137 is prime

Smallest prime with 3 distinct digits that remains prime if one of its digits is removed

Remove 1, 37 is left which is prime

Remove 3, 17 is left which is prime

Remove 7, 13 is left which is prime

$137 = (1 + 3 + 7)^2 + (7 - 3)^2 = 11^2 + 4^2$

$137 = 1 + 3 + 7 + (3 - 1)^7 = 10 + 2^7$

137 * 81103 = 1111111

4 different square consists of 5 digits: 1, 6, 7, 8 and 9

137^2 = 18769,

133^2 = 17689,

281^2 = 78961

286^2 = 81796

14th July

14th July can be expressed as 14/7

Sum of digits of 147 = 1 + 4 + 7 = 12

147 = 12^2 + 1 + 2

147 = 2^0 + 2^1 + 2^4 + 2^7

The first column of mobile number display

1 2 3

4 5 6

7 8 9

147^2 = 21609

216 is a perfect cube of 6

09 is a perfect square of 3

15th July

15th July can be expressed as 15/7

196th (14^2) day of non-leap year (Jan-31, Feb – 28, Mar – 31, Apr -30, May – 31, Jun – 30 & Jul – 15)

169 days (13^2) remain until the end of the year

(365 – 196 = 169)

$157 = 1 + 5 + 7 + 12^2$

Smallest 3-digit number whose square contains the same digits as its successor:

$157^2 = 24649$

$158^2 = 24964$

157 is a prime number

If we reverse the digits of 157, we get 751 which is also prime. Hence 157 is emirp (reverse of prime)

16th July

16th July can be expressed as 16/7

$167 = 13^2 – 2$

Smallest multi-digit prime such that the product of digits is equal to the number of digits times the sum of the digits

$1 \times 6 \times 7 = 3 \times (1 + 6 + 7)$

167 is prime

Drop first digit, 67 remains; 67 is prime

Drop first two digits, 7 remains; 7 is prime

$167^2 = 27889$

The digits 2, 7, 8 and 9 are in ascending order

$127^4 = 777796321$

Smallest number whose 4th power has first 4 same digits

17th July

17th July can be expressed as 17/7

$177 = 2^7 + 7^2$

$177^3 = 5545233$

Cube of 17 consists of digits: 2, 3, 4 and 5

Sum of digits of $177 = 1 + 7 + 7 = 15$

Sum of first 15 primes

$177 = 2 + 3 + 5 + 7 + 11 + 13 + 17 + 19 + 23 + 29 + 31 + 37 + 41 + 43 + 47$

18th July

18th July can be expressed as 18/7

$187 = 94 + 93$

$187 = 94^2 - 93^2$

$187 = 14^2 - 3^2$

$187 = 2^3 + 2^3 + 4^3 + 5^3$

19th July

19th July can be expressed as 19/7

$197 = 2^3 + 3^3 + 4^3$

$197 = 14^2 + 1$

$197 = 99 + 98$

$197 = 99^2 - 98^2$

197 is prime

Drop any digit, what remains is prime

Drop 1, 97 is prime

Drop 9, 17 is prime

Drop 7, 19 is prime

19th July is 200th day of a non-leap year (Jan-31, Feb-28, Mar-31, Apr-30, May-31, Jun-30 and Jul-19)

197 is the sum of the first twelve prime numbers: 2 + 3 + 5 + 7 + 11 + 13 + 17 + 19 + 23 + 29 + 31 + 37

Following are the 2 digit prime numbers

11, 13, 17, 19, 23, 29, 31, 37, 41, 43, 47, 53, 59, 61, 67, 71, 73, 79, 83, 89, 97

If we add them all, what we get is 197

20th July

20th July can be expressed as 20/7

4th Power of 207 consists of 10 digits; First 5 and second 5 consists of same digits; re-arranged

$207^4 = 1836036801$

207 can be expressed using digits 1 to 9; each once

$207 = 89 + 61 + 43 + 7 + 5 + 2$

$207 = 3^2 * 23 = 9 * 23$

21st July

21st July can be expressed as 21/7

$217 = 6^3 + 1$

$217 = (1 + 2 + 3 + 4 + 5)^2 - 2^3$

Sum of digits of 217 = 2 + 1 + 7 = 10

Square of 10 = 100

Factors of 100 are 1, 2, 4, 5, 10, 20, 25 50 and 100

If we add them

$1 + 2 + 4 + 5 + 10 + 20 + 25 + 50 + 100 = 217$

22nd July

22nd July can be expressed as 22/7

22/7 is approximate value of pi

In the novel Life of Pi by Yann Martel, the protagonist (Pi) survives 227 days shipwrecked at sea with a Bengal tiger

227 is 7^2 (49th) prime number

22 + 7 = 29 is prime too

227 = 2 * 3 * 5 * 7 + 2 + 3 + 5 + 7

Product of digits of 227 = 2 * 2 * 7 = 28

28 is a perfect number as sum of its factor excluding itself is 28

28 = 1 + 2 + 4 + 7 + 14

23rd July

23rd July can be expressed as 23/7

Smallest 3-digit number with its digits being 3 different primes that is not prime nor any of the permutations of its digits represent a prime number

2, 3 and 7 all are prime but 237 is not

237 = 3 * 79

Smallest number with the property that its first 3 multiples contain the digit 7

237 * 1 = 237

237 * 2 = 474

237 * 3 = 711

237^2 = 56169 ends in 169 = 13^2

237^4 = 3154956561 ends in 6561 which is 81^2

237 = (2 + 3 + 7) + (1 + 2 + 3 + 4 + 5)^2

24th July

24 * 7 represents 24 hours of the day & 7 days of the week

Smallest number which can be expressed as the difference between two integers that contain together all digits 0 – 9

247 = 50123 – 49876

247 = (2 + 4 + 7) * 19

247 = 13 * 19

1319 is a prime number

1913 is also prime

25th July

25th July can be expressed as 25/7

257 = 2^8 + 1 = 4^4 + 1 = 16^2 + 1

257 is the largest prime number of the form x^x + 1 (4^4 + 1)

253 and 259 are the neighbour prime to 257

(253 + 259)/2 = 257

25th July when written as 25/07 becomes 2507

2507 is a Friedman number; can be expressed using it's digit: 2, 5, 0 and 7 exactly once

$2507 = 50^2 + 7$

26th July

26th July can be expressed as 26/7

$267 = 3 * 89$

$267^2 = 71289$

$289 = 17^2$

4th power of 267 contains "21" 3 times

$267^4 = 5082121521$

$267 = 2^0 + 2^1 + 2^3 + 2^8$

27th July

27th July can be expressed as 27/7

277 is super^3 prime

277 is 59th prime number

59 is 17th prime

17th is 7th prime number

7 is 4th prime number

A pizza can be cut into 277 pieces by using only 23 cuts. 23 is prime too

$277 = (2 + 7)^2 + (7 + 7)^2$

28th July

$287 = (2 + 8 + 7)^2 - \text{sqrt}(28/7) = 17^2 - 2$

$287 = (28 * 7) + (2 + 8 + 7) * 7 = 196 + 91$

$287 = 144 + 143$

$287 = 144^2 - 143^2$

The sum of consecutive primes in 3 different ways:

$287 = 89 + 97 + 101$

$287 = 47 + 53 + 59 + 61 + 67$

$287 = 17 + 19 + 23 + 29 + 31 + 37 + 41 + 43 + 47$

$287 = 2^0 + 2^1 + 2^2 + 2^3 + 2^4 + 2^8$

29th July

29th July can be expressed as 29/7

$297 = 3 * 3 * 33$

$297 = 17^2 + 1 + 7$

If we re-arrange the digits of 297, one of the 3 digits number formed is 729

$729 = 27^2 = 9^3$

$297 = (2 + 9 + 7)^2 - 27$

Both 29 and 7 are prime numbers

$297^2 = 88209$

$88 + 209 = 297$

$297 = 149 + 148$

$297 = 149^2 - 148^2$

If abc is a 3 digit number and the number formed by reversing the digits of abc is cba

$abc - cba = (100a + 10b + c)-(100c + 10b + a) = 99(a-c)$

If $(a-c) = 3$, then we get $99 * 3 = 297$

We can get 60 such numbers

Original Number	Reverse Number	Difference (Original - Reverse)	Original Number	Reverse Number	Difference (Original - Reverse)	Original Number	Reverse Number	Difference (Original - Reverse)
996	699	297	895	598	297	794	497	297
986	689	297	885	588	297	784	487	297
976	679	297	875	578	297	774	477	297
966	669	297	865	568	297	764	467	297
956	659	297	855	558	297	754	457	297
946	649	297	845	548	297	744	447	297
936	639	297	835	538	297	734	437	297
926	629	297	825	528	297	724	427	297
916	619	297	815	518	297	714	417	297
906	609	297	805	508	297	704	407	297

Original Number	Reverse Number	Difference (Original - Reverse)	Original Number	Reverse Number	Difference (Original - Reverse)	Original Number	Reverse Number	Difference (Original - Reverse)
693	396	297	491	194	297	390	93	297
683	386	297	481	184	297	380	83	297
673	376	297	471	174	297	370	73	297
663	366	297	461	164	297	360	63	297
653	356	297	451	154	297	350	53	297
643	346	297	441	144	297	340	43	297
633	336	297	431	134	297	330	33	297
623	326	297	421	124	297	320	23	297
613	316	297	411	114	297	310	13	297
603	306	297	401	104	297	300	3	297

30th July

30th July can be expressed as 30/7

$307 = 17^0 + 17^1 + 17^2$

$307 = 18^2 - 18^1 + 18^0$

$307 = 3 * (3 + 0 + 7) + 7$

$307 = 7^3 - 6^2$

$307 = 154 + 153$

$307 = 154^2 - 153^2$

$307^2 = 94249$

94249 is a palindrome

307 is prime

37 is prime

7 is prime

The following equation consists of all prime numbers adding to give another prime. All digits: 0 to 9 are used here

$307 = 2 + 5 + 41 + 67 + 83 + 109$

If we reverse 307, we get 703

$703^2 = 494209$

Adding first half and second half of 494209 = 494 + 209 = 703

31st July

31st July can be expressed as 31/7

317 is prime

173, 137, 13, 31, 37, 73, 17, 71, 7 and 3 are prime

Sum of digits of 317 = 3 + 1 + 7 = 11 is prime

Sum of square of its digits is 59 is prime

$3^2 = 9$, $1^1 = 1$ and $7^2 = 49$

$317 = (-3)^3 + 1^3 + 7^3$

$317 = 18^2 - 8 + 1$

August

1st August

1st August can be expressed as 1/8

Only positive number that is twice the sum of its digits

$18 = 2 * (1 + 8)$

Sum of digits of 18 = 1 + 8 = 9 is perfect square of 3

$18 = 3^3 - 3^2$

$18 = 3 + 4 + 5 + 6$

$18^2 = 324$

$324^2 = 104976$

324 and 104976 contains all digits 0 to 9 once

$18^3 = 5832$

Sum of digits of 5832 = 5 + 8 + 3 + 2 = 18

2nd August

2nd August can be expressed as 2/8

Only 2-digit number which is perfect

28 is a perfect number as sum of its factors (excluding itself) is the number itself

8128 is only 4 digit perfect number

$8128 = 1 + 2 + 4 + 8 + 16 + 32 + 64 + 127 + 254 + 508 + 1016 + 2032 + 4064$

$28 = 1 + 2 + 4 + 7 + 14$

Sum of first 7 natural numbers

$28 = 1 + 2 + 3 + 4 + 5 + 6 + 7$

$28 = 5^2 + 5 - 2$

The following equation contain all digits 1 to 9 once

$28 \times 157 = 4396$

Calendar repeats after every 28 years

3rd August

3rd August can be expressed as 3/8

Sum of squares of first 3 prime numbers

$38 = 2^3 + 3^2 + 5^2$

$38 = 3 + 8 + 3^3$

$38^2 = 1444$

Only 4-digit perfect square (containing no zeroes) having last 3 digits same

4th August

4th August can be expressed as 4/8

$48 = 6^2 + 6 * 2$

The following equation contain all digits 1 to 9; each once

48 x 159 = 7632

Smallest number with 10 proper divisors (1, 2, 3, 4, 6, 8, 12, 16, 24 and 48)

$48 = 13^2 - 11^2 = 8^2 - 4^2 = 7^2 - 1^2$

$48 = (4 * 8) + 4 + 8 + 4$

$48 = (4^3 + 8^3) / (4 + 8)$

5th August

5th August can be expressed as 5/8

$58 = 2^6 - 6$

Sum of the first seven prime numbers:

$58 = 2 + 3 + 5 + 7 + 11 + 13 + 17$

$58 = 2 * 29$

$5 + 8 = 2 + 2 + 9$

6th August

6th August can be expressed as 6/8

Smallest composite number that becomes prime by turning it upside down

$68 = 4^3 + 4$

$68 = 6 * 8 + 6 + 8 + 6$

68 is the last two-digit number to appear in the digits of pi

$6^2 + 8^2 = 100$

Last day of November 46 B.C. was the longest day in history, it lasted 68 days

7th August

7th August can be expressed as 7/8

$78 = 7 * 8 + 7 + 8 + 7$

$78 = 9^2 - 9^1/2$

Sum of first 12 natural numbers

$78 = 1 + 2 + 3 + 4 + 5 + 6 + 7 + 8 + 9 + 10 + 11 + 12$

8th August

8th August can be expressed as 8/8

$88^2 = 7744$

Square of 88 consist of 2 two-digits number 77 and 44

Same upside down or when viewed in a mirror

Eighty eight, 11 letters long, is the longest number that is normally typed using strictly alternating hands

$88 = 2 * 2 * 22$

$88 = 8 * 8 + 8 + 8 + 8$

$100 = 8 * 8 + 8 + 8 + 8 + 88/8 + 8^0$

1000 = 888 + 88 + 8 + 8 + 8

Approximately the number of days it takes Mercury to complete its orbit

9th August

9th August can be expressed as 9/8

$98 = 9 + 8 + 9 * 9$

$98 = 1^4 + 2^4 + 3^4$

Normal body temperature is 98.6 degrees Fahrenheit

Smallest number which has its first 5 multiple contain 9

$98 * 1 = 098$

$98 * 2 = 196$

$98 * 3 = 294$

$98 * 4 = 392$

$98 * 5 = 490$

$98^2 = 9604$

If we re-arrange the digits of 9604 to get 4096

$4096 = 64^2 = 16^3$

With every increase in power of 98, first two digits decrease by 2 from 96 to 94, 92, 90 and so on

$98^2 = 9604$

$98^3 = 94112$

98^3 = 92236816

98^4 = 9039207968

August 9 is the 222nd day of the year in a leap year

144 (12^2) days remain until the end of the year

10th August

10th August can be expressed as 10/8

$108 = 1^1 * 2^2 * 3^3$

$108 = (1 + 0 + 8) * (10 + 8^1/3)$

$108 = (1 + 0 + 8)^2 + (1 + 0 + 8) * 2 + (1 + 0 + 8)^1$

August 10 is the 222nd day of the year in a non-leap year

144 (12^2) days remain until the end of the year

Diameter of the Sun = 108 * Diameter of the Earth

If we put the neighbours of 108 (107 and 109) with 108, 108107 and 108109 are prime numbers

11th August

11th August can be expressed as 11/8

$118 = 11^2 - 8^1/3$

$118 = (1 + 1 + 8)^2 + 11 + 8 - 1$

$118 = 2^8 - (1 + 1 + 8)$

Sum of digits of 1 + 1 + 8 = 10 = 1 + 0 = 1

$118^2 = 13924$

$1 + 3 + 9 + 2 + 4 = 19 = 1 + 9 = 10 = 1 + 0 = 1$

$118^3 = 1643032$

$1643032 = 1 + 6 + 4 + 3 + 0 + 3 + 2 = 19 = 1 + 9 = 10 = 1 + 0 = 1$

$118^4 = 193877776$

$1 + 9 + 3 + 8 + 7 + 7 + 7 + 7 + 6 = 55 = 5 + 5 = 10 + 1 + 0 = 1$

12th August

12th August can be expressed as 12/8

$128 = 2^{(8 - 1)}$

Smallest 3 digit Friedman's Number (Can be expressed using it's own digit once)

$128 = (8 - 2 - 1)^3 + 8^1/3$

$128 = (1 * 2) + (1 * 2 * 3) + (1 * 2 * 3 * 4 * 5) = 2! + 3! + 5!$

Product of its digit = $1 * 2 * 8 = 16 = 4^2$

$128 = 9 + 11 + 13 + 15 + 17 + 19 + 21 + 23$

Largest number which is not the sum of distinct squares

28 is a perfect number

8128 is a perfect number

13th August

13th August can be expressed as 13/8

$138 = 2 * 3 * 23$

$138 = (1 + 3 + 8)^2 - [(1 + 3 + 8)/2]$

$138 = 2^7 + 1 + 2 + 3 + 4$

$138 = 5^3 + 13$

$138 = 5! + 4! - 3!$

August 13 is the 225th day of the year (226th in leap years) in the Gregorian calendar

$225 = (1 + 2 + 3 + 4 + 5)^2$

14th August

14th August can be expressed as 14/8

$148 = (1 + 4 + 8)^2 - (4^0 + 4^1 + 4^2)$

$1 = 2^0, 4 = 2^2$ and $8 = 2^3$

$148 = 12^2 + 4^1/2 + 8^1/3$

$1 * 4 * 8 = 32 = 2^{(8 - 4 + 1)}$

15th August

15th August can be expressed as 15/8

$158 = 2 * (2^7 - 7^2)$

$158 = 2 * [(7 * 9) + (7 + 9)]$

$158 = 1 + 5 + 8 + 12^2$

$158 = \sim 2 * 8.888^2$

The major angle formed at 8 minutes passed 15 (3 PM) is 314. The first three digits of value of pi

16th August

16th August can be expressed as 16/8

$168 = (8 + 6 - 1)^2 - 168^0$

$1 + 6 + 8 = 1 + 2 + 3 + 4 + 5$

$168 = 4^1/2 * (4^1 + 4^2 + 4^3)$

$168 = 2 * (2^5 + 3^3 + 5^2)$

$168 = 24 * 7 = 168$ hours in a week

$169^7 - 169$ is divisible by 168

$(n^7 - n$ is divisible by 168 when n is odd)

$168 = 6 * 28$

Both 6 and 28 are perfect number

$6 = 1 + 2 + 3$

$28 = 1 + 2 + 4 + 7 + 14$

Square of 168 consists of only 3 digits which are individually power of 2

$2 = 2^1, 4 = 2^2$ and $8 = 2^3$

$168^2 = 28224$

There are 168 primes less than 1000

17th August

17th August can be expressed as 17/8

Sum of digits = 1 + 7 + 8 = 16 is a perfect square

17 + 8 = 25 is a perfect square too

178 in base 10 = (10110010) in base 2 consists of equal number of 0's and 1's

$(178)_{10} = (10110010)_2$

Squares and cubes of 178 and 196 are strongly related as they consist of same digits

$178^2 = 31,684$

$196^2 = 38,416$

$178^3 = 5,639,752$

$196^3 = 7,529,536$

$178 = 2^1 * (2^3 + 3^4)$

$178 = 13^2 + 1 * 3^2$

18th August

18th August can be expressed as 18/8

Express 188 using eight 8's

$188 = 8 * 8 + 8 * 8 + 8 * 8 - 8^1/3 - 8^1/3$

Square of 188 consist of 3 digits: 3, 4 and 5

$188^2 = 35344$

$188 = 48^2 - 46^2$

Each digit individually is a perfect cube: 1, 8 and 8

19th August

19th August can be expressed as 19/8

$198 = (1 + 9 + 8) * 11$

$198 = 11 + 99 + 88$

$198 = 11 + 88 + 99 = 22 + 77 + 99 = 33 + 66 + 99 = 44 + 55 + 99$

If abc is a 3 digit number and the number formed by reversing the digits of abc is cba

$abc - cba = (100a + 10b + c)-(100c + 10b + a) = 99(a-c)$

If (a-c) = 2, then we get $99 * 2 = 198$

We can get 70 such numbers

20th August

20th August can be expressed as 20/8

$208 = 2 * (2 + 0 + 8)^2 + 8$

$208 = 2^3 * 3^3 - 2^3$

Sum of squares of first 5 prime numbers

$208 = 2^2 + 3^2 + 5^2 + 7^2 + 11^2$

$208 = 2 * 2^3 + 3 * 4^3$

$2 + 0 + 8 = 10 = 1 + 0 = 1$

$208^2 = 43264$

$4 + 3 + 2 + 6 + 4 = 19 = 1 + 9 = 10 = 1 + 0 = 1$

21st August

21st August can be expressed as 21/8

$218 = 6^3 + 6/3$

$218 = (1 + 2 + 3 + 4 + 5)^2 - (2^0 + 2^1 + 2^2)$

$218 = 2^1 + 2^3 + 2^4 + 2^6 + 2^7$

$218 = 2 * (1 * 2 + 3 * 4 + 5 * 6 + 7 * 8 + 9)$

$218 = 2 * (1^1 + 2^2 * 3^3)$

$2 = 2^1, 1 = 2^0$ and $8 = 2^3$

22nd August

22nd August can be expressed as 22/8

$228 = 3^5 - 3 * 5$

$228 = 2^8 - 28$

$228 = 2 + 2 + 8 + 2^3 * 3^3$

$228 = 8^2 + 6^2 + 2^7$

Sum of 10 consecutive prime numbers

$228 = 7 + 11 + 13 + 17 + 19 + 23 + 29 + 31 + 37 + 41$

23rd August

23rd August can be expressed as 23/8

$238 = (23 - 8)^2 + 2 + 3 + 8$

$238 = 3^5 - 5$

$2 + 3 + 8 = 13$ (prime)

$23 + 8 = 31$ (reverse ⊕ prime)

238 can be expressed as sum of FIRST 13 prime numbers

$2 + 3 + 5 + 7 + 11 + 13 + 17 + 19 + 23 + 29 + 31 + 37 + 41$

Square of 238 consist of 3 digits: 4, 5 and 6

$238^2 = 56644$

24th August

24th August can be expressed as 24/8

Each digit of 248 consists of first three power of 2

$2 = 2^1, 4 = 2^2$ and $8 = 2^3$

$24 + 8 = 32 = 2^5$

$2 * 4 * 8 = 64 = 2^6$

$248 = 3^5 + 5$

$248 = 2^8 - 8$

If 24 August is written as 2408

$2408 = 7^4 + 7^1 = 2401 + 7$

25th August

25th August can be expressed as 25/8

$258 = 6^1 + 6^2 + 6^3$

$258 = 4^4 + 4^1/2$

$258 = 3^5 + 3 * 5$

$258 = 2^8 + 8^1/3$

$258 = 25 * 8 + 58$

258^2 consists of 3 digits 4, 5 and 6

$258^2 = 66564$

258 is the **middle column** of mobile number display

1 2 3

4 5 6

7 8 9

If 25th August is written as 25/08,

$2508 = 50^2 + 8$

(Friedman Number)- Can be expressed using 2, 5, 0 and 8 exactly once

26th August

26th August can be expressed as 26/8

$268 = (2 + 6 + 8)^1/4 * (1^3 + 2^3 + 5^3)$

$268 = 3^5 + 5^2$

$268 = 2 + 8 + 6^1 + 6^2 + 6^3$

$268 = 2^2 * (68 - 1)$

Smallest number whose product of digits is 6 times the sum of its digits

$2 * 6 * 8 = 6(2 + 6 + 8)$

$96 = 6 * 16$

27th August

27th August can be expressed as 27/8

$278 = 3^5 + 35$

$278 = 2 * 139 \ (1 = 3^0, 3 = 3^1 \text{ and } 9 = 3^2)$

28th August

28th August can be expressed as 28/8

$288 = 1^1 + 2^2 + 3^3 + 4^4$

$288 = (2 * 8)^2 + 2 * 8 * 2$

$288 = 1 * (1 * 2) * (1 * 2 * 3) * (1 * 2 * 3 * 4) = 1! * 2! * 3! * 4!$

$288 = 2 * 12^2$

$288 * 882 = 504^2$

$288 = 17^2 - 17^0$

$288 = 324 - 32 - 4$

$288 = (2 + 8 + 8)^2 - 2 * (2 + 8 + 8)$

29th August

29th August can be expressed as 29/8

241st day of the year starting from 1st Jan

If we reverse the digits of 241, we get 142; that's the number of days remaining for the year

$298 = 2 * 149$

1, 4, 9 is the square of first 3 natural numbers: 1, 2 and 3

$298 = 2 * (6^2 + 7^2 + 8^2)$

$298 = (2 + 9 + 8)^2 - 4^4 - 1$

First 3 digits of square of 298 is 8. The only 3-digit number to have so

$298^2 = 88804$

30th August

30th August can be expressed as 30/8

$308 = 280 + 28 + 0$

308 = (3 + 0 + 8) * 4 * 7

$308 = 18^2 - 8 - 8$

$308 = 7^3 - 7 * 5$

308 + 803 = 1111

123 days remain until the end of the year

31st August

31st August can be expressed as 31/8

$318 = 18^2 - $ sqrt (18 * 2)

$318 = 7^3 - 5^2$

3 * 1 * 8 = 2 * (3 + 1 + 8)

3 * 1 * 8 = 24

3 + 1 + 8 = 12

318 can be expressed as sum of 12 prime numbers

318 = 7 + 11 + 13 + 17 + 19 + 23 + 29 + 31 + 37 + 41 + 43 + 47

September

1ˢᵗ September

1ˢᵗ September can be expressed as 1/9

$19 = 1 * 9 + 1 + 9$

$19 = 4! - 3! + 2! + 1!$

Smallest prime with the following pattern

19

197

1979

19793

197933

1979339

19793393

197933933

1979339339

$19 = XIX$ (Roman)

19 is the largest prime number to be palindrome in Roman

$19 = 32 - 3^2 - 2^2$

$19 = 53 - 5^2 - 3^2$

$19 = 72 - 7^2 - 2^2$

Sum of first 19 natural number is 190

1 + 2 + 3 + ... + 19 = 19 * 10

Any number of the form

abcdefghiabcdefghi is perfectly divisible by 19

For example

987654321987654321 is perfectly divisible by 19

29 = 2 * 9 + 2 + 9

39 = 3 * 9 + 3 + 9

49 = 4 * 9 + 4 + 9

59 = 5 * 9 + 5 + 9

69 = 6 * 9 + 6 + 9

79 = 7 * 9 + 7 + 9

89 = 8 * 9 + 8 + 9

99 = 9 * 9 + 9 + 9

80! = 80 * 79 * 78 * ... * 3 * 2 * 1, end in 19 Zeroes

19 = 3 * 6 + 1

19^2 = 361

2nd September

2nd September can be expressed as 2/9

29 = 2 * 9 + 2 + 9

29 = 2 * 5 + 3 * 3 + 5 * 2 (253->352)

29 = 2^2 + 3^2 + 4^2

A pizza can be cut into 29 pieces by just $(9 - 2)$ 7 cuts

In the DD-MM-YYYY format, there are 29 palindromic dates in 21st century

Following are few to start with

10-Feb-2001 (10022001),

20-Feb-2002 (20022002),

1-Feb-2010 (01022010),

11-Feb-2011 (11022011),

21-Feb-2012 (21022012)

And so on...

$29^2 = 841$ ($8 = 2^3$, $4 = 2^2$ and $1 = 2^0$)

3rd September

3rd September can be expressed as 3/9

$39 = 6^2 + 6/2$

$39 = 3^1 + 3^2 + 3^3$

$39 = 3 * 13$

39 can be expressed as sum of prime using primes between (including) 3 and 13

$39 = 3 + 5 + 7 + 11 + 13$

$39 * 31 = 13 * 93$

$39 * 62 = 26 * 93$

39 * 93 = 39 * 93

The following equation contain digits 1 to 9, exactly once

39 x 186 = 7254

Cube root of 39 is approximate 3.39

39 weeks = gestation period for human beings

4th September

4th September can be expressed as 4/9

49 is a perfect square of 7

4 is perfect square of 2

9 is perfect square of 3

4 * 9 = 36 is a perfect square of 6

9/4 = 2.25 is a perfect square of 1.5

Smallest number with the property that it and its neighbours are squareful (Contains at-least one square in prime factorization)

$48 = 4^2$ x 3,

$49 = 7^2$ x 1,

$50 = 5^2$ x 2

$49^2 = 2401$

Sum of digits of 2401 = 2 + 4 + 0 + 1 = 7

Cube of 49 ends in 49

$49^3 = 117649$

4th power of 49 and 32 share the same digits

$49^4 = 5764801$

$32^4 = 1048576$

$49 = 4 * 9 + 4 + 9$

49 is sum of first 7 odd numbers

$49 = 1 + 3 + 5 + 7 + 9 + 11 + 13$

$49 = 47 + 2$ and $94 = 47 * 2$

$499 = 497 + 2$ and $994 = 497 * 2$

$4999 = 497 + 2$ and $9994 = 4997 * 2$

5th September

5th September can be expressed as 5/9

$59 = 5 * 9 + 5 + 9$

59 gives a remainder of 1, 2, 3, 4 and 5 when divided by 2, 3, 4, 5 and 6

59 is the 17th prime

17 is 7th prime

7 is 4th prime

1 Day on Mercury = 59 Days on Earth

It is possible to see as much as 59% of the Moon's surface from the Earth

September 5 is the 248th day of the year (249th in leap years) in the Gregorian calendar

118 days remain (including 5th September) until the end of the year

$118 = 2 * 59$

6th September

6th September can be expressed as 6/9

$69 = 6 * 9 + 6 + 9$

$69 = 66 + 3$

$69 = 6 * 6 + 33$

Square and Cube; when combined, captures each digit from 0 to 9; exactly once

$69^2 = 4761$

$69^3 = 328509$

69 when turned upside down becomes 69 (such numbers are called Strobogrammatic numbers)

7th September

7th September can be expressed as 7/9

$79 = 7 * 9 + 7 + 9$

$79 = 2^7 - 7^2$

79 is prime and if we reverse to get 97, is also prime

79 = 11 + 31 + 37 (Sum of 3 primes)

97 = 11 + 13 + 73 (Sum of prime; reversed for 31 and 37)

Sum of digits of 79 = 7 + 9 = 16 = 8 + 8

Square root of 79 is 8.888

Atomic number of gold is 79

8th September

8th September can be expressed as 8/9

$89 = 8^1 + 9^2$

$89 = 8 * 9 + 8 + 9$

$89 = 9 + 8 + 7 + 6 + 5 + 4 + 3 + 2 + 1 + 2 + 3 + 4 + 5 + 6 + 7 + 8 + 9$

$8989^2 = 80802121$

$89^3 = 7921$

If we re-arrange 7921 to get 2197 = 13^3

Hellin's Law states that every 89th pregnancy result in twins, every 89^2 pregnancy result in triplets and every 89^3 pregnancy result in quadruplets

9th September

9th September can be expressed as 9/9

$99 = 9 * 9 + 9 + 9$

$99 = 3 * 33$

$99 = 10^2 - 10^0$

$99 = 2^3 + 3^3 + 4^3$

$99 = 98 + 01$

$99^2 = 9801$

Sum of digits of $99 = 9 + 9 = 18$

Sum of digits of $9801 = 18$

$99 = 2 * 7^2 + 1$

$99^2 = 2 * 70^2 + 1$

Square root of 99 is 9.9

$1/99 = 1.010101..\%$

Highest 2-digit number in decimal system

Atomic number of Einsteinium is 99

10th September

10th September can be expressed as 10/9

$109 = 10 * 9 + 10 + 9$

$109 = 1^1 + 2^2 * 3^3$

$109 = 12 * 3^2 + 1$ (palindrome $1 - 2 - 3 - 2 - 1$)

Square of 109 consist of only 2 digits which are perfect cube: 1 and 8

$109^2 = 11881$

$109 = 118 - 8 - 1$

109 = 1 + 29 + 50 + 29

109^3 = 1295029

109 = 1 * 2 + 3 * 4 + 5 * 6 + 7 * 8 + 9

$109^{1/5}$ = 2.5555...

109 along with 601 are the only invertible primes that appear on a digital clock

Soap bubbles can only join each other at one or two angles: 109 or 120 degrees. No other angles are possible

11th September

11th September can be expressed as 11/9

119 = 11 * 9 + 11 + 9

119 = 5 * 4 * 3 * 2 * 1 − 119^0

119 = 3^4 + 3^3 + 3^2 + 3^1 − 3^0

119 = $(1 + 1 + 9)^2$ − 1 − 1

119 = 2^7 − 2 − 7

119 = 7 * 17

7 and 17 both are prime ending in 7

1 + 1 + 9 = 11 is also prime

If we reverse the digits of 119, we get 911. 911 is also prime

If we drop any one digit from 119, what remains is prime

If we drop 1, 19 remains which is prime

If we drop 9, 11 remains which is also prime

119 is concatenation of 5th prime (11) and 5th composite (9) number

September 11 being the 254th day of the non-leap year has 111 days remain until the end of the year

12th September

12th September can be expressed as 12/9

$129 = 12 * 9 + 12 + 9$

$129 = 1^7 + 2^7$

$129 = (1 + 2 + 9)^2 - (1 + 2 + 3 + 4 + 5)$

$129 = 5^3 + [(5 + 3)/2]$

$129 = 11^2 + 9 - 1$

$129 = 3 * 43$

$343 = 7^3$

129 can be expressed as sum of first 10 prime numbers or sum of all prime till 29

$129 = 2 + 3 + 5 + 7 + 11 + 13 + 17 + 19 + 23 + 29$

Smallest number to be expressed as the sum of 3 squares in 4 ways

$129 = 1^2 + 8^2 + 8^2$

$129 = 2^2 + 2^2 + 11^2$

$129 = 2^2 + 5^2 + 10^2$

$129 = 4^2 + 7^2 + 8^2$

13th September

13th September can be expressed as 13/9

139 can be expressed in first 3 powers of 3

$1 = 3^0$, $3 = 3^1$ and $9 = 3^2$

$1 * 3 * 9 = 27 = 3^3$

$139 = 2^2 + 3^2 + 4^2 + 5^2 + 6^2 + 7^2$

139 is the smallest prime number whose product of digits give a perfect cube

Smallest prime that contains one prime digit (3), one composite digit(9), and one digit that is neither prime nor composite (1)

$139 = 9 * 8 + 7 * 6 + 5 * 4 + 3 * 2 - 1$

The next prime after 139 is 149 which is 10 away. This is the first pair of prime number of have difference of 10.

Square of 139 ends in 321 and begins with digits 193 (re-arranged 139)

$139^2 = 19321$

The famous Ramanujan Magic Square gives sum of any row/column/corners/centre as 139

22	12	18	87
88	17	9	25
10	24	89	16
19	86	23	11

Take Any Row

22 + 12 + 18 + 87 = 139

88 + 17 + 9 + 25 = 139

10 + 24 + 89 + 16 = 139

19 + 86 + 23 + 11 = 139

Take Any Column

22 + 88 + 10 + 19 = 139

12 + 17 + 24 + 86 = 139

18 + 9 + 89 + 23 = 139

87 + 25 + 16 + 11 = 139

Sum of both diagonals is also 139

22 + 17 + 89 + 11 = 139

87 + 9 + 24 + 19 = 139

Sum of all corner numbers is also 139

22 + 87 + 19 + 11 = 139

Sum of centred numbers is also 139

17 + 9 + 24 + 89 = 139

And others... combinations

The first row of this magic square

22.12.1887 (22nd December 1887) is the birthdate of Srinivas Ramanujan

14th September

14th September can be expressed as 14/9

Digits of 149 individually are squares of 1, 2 and 3 respectively

$1 = 1^2$, $4 = 2^2$ and $9 = 3^2$

$149 = 14 * 9 + 14 + 9$

$149 = 6^2 + 7^2 + 8^2$

$149 = 12^2 + 14 - 9$

149 is a prime number. The previous prime to 149 is 139 which is 10 away. This is the first pair of prime number of have difference of 10.

If we reverse the digits of 149, we get 941 which is also prime

Between 1 and 9, there are 4 primes

Square of 149 consists of 3 consecutive digits: 0, 1 and 2

149 is the smallest number to have a square whose first 3 digits are 222

$149^2 = 22201$

$(1 + 4 + 9)/2 = 2 + 2 + 2 + 0 + 1$

15th September

15th September can be expressed as 15/9

$159 = 15 * 9 + 15 + 9$

$159 = 15^2 - 9^2 + 1 + 5 + 9$

159 = 3 * 53 (product of two primes)

159 = 47 + 53 + 59

159 = 3 * (5 + 7 + 11 + 13 + 17)

$159 = 2^0 + 2^1 + 2^2 + 2^3 + 2^4 + 2^7$

159 is the **diagonal** of mobile number display

1 2 3

4 5 6

7 8 9

16th September

16th September can be expressed as 16/9

169 is a perfect square whose digits are in ascending order

$169 = 13^2$

$961 = 31^2$ (reverse the digits to get square reversed)

If we re-arrange the digits of 169, we get $196 = 14^2 = (9 + 6 - 1)^2$

$1 + 6 + 9 = 16 = 4^2 = (9 - 6 + 1)^2$

$13^2 = 12^2 + 5^2$

169 = 16 * 9 + 16 + 9

$169 = 8^3 - 7^3$

$169 = 2 * (3^2 + 2^2)$

$169^{1/2} = 19 - 6$

17th September

17th September can be expressed as 17/9

$179 = 17 * 9 + 17 + 9$

$179 = 14^2 - 1 - 7 - 9$

179 is a prime number

971 (reverse of 179) is prime too

179 days out of 365 days of a non-leap year are even

Square of 179 consist of digit 0 to 4; each once

$179^2 = 32041$

18th September

18th September can be expressed as 18/9

$189 = 18 * 9 + 18 + 9$

$189 = 14^2 - 14/2$

$189 = 4^3 + 5^3$

If we write down all digits from 1 to 99, the digit formed will have 189 digits

$12345678910111213...99 = 189$ digits

Prime quadruplet is a set of 4 primes of the form a, a + 2, a + 6, and a + 8

Product of 4 primes in a prime quadruplet (except for 5, 7, 11, 13) always ends in 189

For example:

11 x 13 x 17 x 19 = 46,189

189 in base 10 is palindrome in base 2 – 10111101

$(189)_{10}$ = $(10111101)_2$

19th September

19th September can be expressed as 19/9

199 = 19 * 9 + 19 + 9

Sum of digits of 199 = 1 + 9 + 9 = 19

199^2 = 39601

Sum of digits of 39601 = 3 + 9 + 6 + 0 + 1 = 19

Product of digits of 199 = 1 * 9 * 9 = 81 = 9^2

199 can be expressed as sum of squares of number starting from 3

$199 = 3^2 + 4^2 + 5^2 + 6^2 + 7^2 + 8^2$

199 can be expressed as sum of square of first 5 prime number (excluding 3)

$199 = 2^2 + 5^2 + 7^2 + 11^2$

199 is prime and if we turned it upside down, we get 661 which is prime too

Re-arrange 199, to get 991. 991 is prime

Re-arrange 199, to get 919. 919 is prime

199 is the largest part of a prime quadruplet: 191, 193, 197, 199

20th September

20th September can be expressed as 20/9

$209 = 20 * 9 + 20 + 9$

$209 = 1^6 + 2^5 + 3^4 + 4^3 + 5^2 + 6^1$

$209 = (20 - 9)(10 + 9)$

$209 = (15 + 4)(15 - 4)$

$209 = 2 * 3 * 5 * 7 - 1$ (Kummer Number)

$88 + 209 = 297$ and $88,209 = 297^2$

Smallest number that can be expressed in six ways as a sum of 3 squares:

$209 = 1^2 + 8^2 + 12^2$

$209 = 2^2 + 3^2 + 14^2$

$209 = 2^2 + 6^2 + 13^2$

$209 = 3^2 + 10^2 + 10^2$

$209 = 4^2 + 7^2 + 12^2$

$209 = 8^2 + 8^2 + 9^2$

21st September

21st September can be expressed as 21/9

$219 = 21 * 9 + 21 + 9$

$219 = (1 + 2 + 3 + 4 + 5)^2 - (9 - 1 - 2)$

$219 = 6^3 + \sqrt{(6 + 3)}$

$219 = 3^3 + 3 * 4^3$

219^2 end in 31^2

$219^2 = 47961$

22nd September

22nd September can be expressed as 22/9

$229 = 22 * 9 + 22 + 9$

$229 = 4^4 - 3^3$

$229 = 2 + 2 + 9 + 6 * 6 * 6$

$229 = 2 + 2 + (9 + 6)^2$

Smallest prime that, when added to the reverse yields another prime: $229 + 922 = 1151$

$2 * 2 * 9 = 36 = 6^2$

$6 * 2 = 12$ and cube root of 12 is 2.29

$229^2 = 52441$ and 441 is square of 21

2209 is a perfect square of 47

September 22 is the 265th day of the year (266th in leap years) in the Gregorian calendar. A century (100) days remain until the end of the year

23rd September

23rd September can be expressed as 23/9

$239 = 23 * 9 + 23 + 9$

$239 = 3^5 - 4$

$239 = 4^4 - 4^2 - 4^0$

$239 = 2 + 3 + 9 + (2 + 3 + 9 + 1)^2$

$239 = (9 - 3)^3 + 23$

239^2 end in 11^2

$239^2 = 57121$

24th September

24th September can be expressed as 24/9

$249 = 24 * 9 + 24 + 9$

$249 = (2 + 4 + 9)^2 + 2^0 + 4^1 + 9^1$

$249 = 2^1 + 3^5 + 4^1$

$249 = 3 * (3^2 + 5^2 + 7^2)$

249^2 end in perfect square and perfect cube

$249^2 = 62001$

$2409 = 49^2 + 2^3$

25th September

25th September can be expressed as 25/9

$259 = 25 * 9 + 25 + 9$

$259 = 6^0 + 6^1 + 6^2 + 6^3$

$259 = (2 + 5 + 9)^0 + (2 + 5 + 9)^{1/4} + (2 + 5 + 9)^2$

$259 = 7 * 37$

7 and 37 both are prime and there are 7 primes between 7 and 37

$7 = 2 + 5 = 3 + 4$

$259 = 7 * (2^2 + 2^2 + 2^2 + 5^2)$

$259 = 7 * (4^3 - 3^3)$

Square of 259 end in 9^2

$259^2 = 67081$

2509 is a Friedman number. 2509 can be expressed using digit 2, 5, 0 and 9, exactly once

$2509 = 50^2 + 9$

26th September

26th September can be expressed as 26/9

269 is the 269th day of the non-leap year starting with 1st Jan as 1st day of the year

$269 = 26 * 9 + 26 + 9$

4th power of 269 end in 4321

269^4 = 5236114321

Longest official game of chess on record of 269 moves took on 12/2/89 Interesting thing to be noted that all the digits of the date (2, 17, 89) are prime numbers

269 is prime too

269^2 = 72361

7, 23 and 61 are prime

27th September

27th September can be expressed as 27/9

279 = 27 * 9 + 27 + 9

Smallest number whose product of digits is 7 times the sum of its digits

2 * 7 * 9 = 7 * (2 + 7 + 9)

279 = 3 * 93 = 3 * 3 * 31 = 3^2 * 31

279 can be expressed as the sum of a prime raised to first 3 primes: 2, 3 and 5

279 = 3^2 + 3^3 + 3^5

279 = 3 * [(5 − 3)^2 + 5^2 + (5 + 3)^2]

28th September

28th September can be expressed as 28/9

289 can be expressed using its own digit exactly once (Friedman's number)

$289 = (8 + 9)^2$

289 a perfect square with its digits in ascending order

289 can be expressed as square of sum of first 4 primes

$289 = (2 + 3 + 5 + 7)^2$

2809 is a perfect square of 53

$2 * 8 * 9 = 144 = 12^2$

$289 = 28 * 9 + 28 + 9$

289 can be expressed as 1, 2, 3 and 4th power of 1, 2, 3 and 4 respectively

$289 = 1^1 + 2^2 + 3^3 + 4^4$

$289^2 = 83521$

$2 + 8 + 9 = 8 + 3 + 5 + 2 + 1$

29th September

29th September can be expressed as 29/9

$299 = 29 * 9 + 29 + 9$

$2 + 9 + 9 = 20$

299 is the smallest number whose sum of digits is 20

$299 = 23 * (2^2 + 3^2)$

$299 = 17^2 + 1 + 7 + 2$

$299 = (1^4 + 2^3 + 3^2 + 4^1 + 5^0)(7^2 - 6^2)$

$299 = 13 * 23$ (product of two primes)

Square of 299 is 17.29

1729 is the famous Ramanujan Number

There are 299 composite number less than 100 which are product of two primes. 299 is one of them

By just applying a dozen straight cuts, a cake can be sliced into 299 pieces

30th September

30th September can be expressed as 30/9

$309 = 30 * 9 + 30 + 9$

Smallest number whose 5th power contains all digits: 0 to 9

$309^5 = 2817036000549$

$309 = 3 * (2^2 + 5^2 + 5^2 + 7^2)$

$309 = 17^2 + 17 + 2 + 1$

$309 = 343 - 34$

October

1st October

1st October can be expressed as 1/10

$110 = 11^2 - 11^1$

$110 = 5^2 + 6^2 + 7^2$

$110 = 2 * (1 + 2 + 3 + 4 + 5 + 6 + 7 + 8 + 9 + 10)$

$110 = 2 * 55 = 22 * 5$

$110 = 5^3 - 5 * 3$

$110 = 11 * 10 = 10 * (10 + 1)$

$110 = (5 * 4 * 3 * 2 * 1)-(4 + 3 + 2 + 1)$

Sum of first 10 even number is 110

$110 = 2 + 4 + 6 + 8 + 10 + 12 + 14 + 16 + 18 + 20$

2nd October

2nd October can be expressed as 2/10

$210 = 21 * 10$

210 is the product of first 4 primes

$210 = 2 * 3 * 5 * 7$

$210 = 14^2 + 14$

$210 = 15^2 - 15$

Sum of first 20 even numbers is 210

Sum of first 20 natural numbers is 210

3rd October

3rd October can be expressed as 3/10

$310 = 31 * 10$

$310 = 3^5 + 3^4 - 3^3 + 3^2 + 3^1 + 3^0$

$310 = 2 * 5 * (2^5 - 1)$

$310 = (5^0 + 5^1 + 5^2) * 10$

$310 = 5 * 2 * (2^0 + 2^1 + 2^2 + 2^3 + 2^4)$

310 in base 10 = 1234 in base 6

$(310)_{10} = (1234)_6$

4th October

4th October can be expressed as 4/10

$410 = 41 * 10$

$410 = (4^2 + 5^2) * 10$

Square of 410 contains 410 at its centre

$410^2 = 44100$

Smallest number that can be expressed as the sum of 2 distinct primes in 2 ways:

$410 = 199 + 211$ and

410 = 97 + 313

Smallest number that can be represented as the sum of the squares of two distinct primes in two different ways

$410 = 7^2 + 19^2$

$410 = 11^2 + 17^2$

Square-root of 410 is 20.25 which is perfect square of 4.5

5th October

5th October can be expressed as 5/10

$510 = 51 * 10$

$510 = 2^1 + 2^2 + 2^3 + 2^4 + 2^5 + 2^6 + 2^7 + 2^8$

$510 = 5 * 3 * 2 (5 * 3 + 2)$

$510 = 8^3 - 8^{1/3}$

$510 = 24^2 + 2^2 + 4^2 + 2^1 + 4^1$

510^3 contains 510

$510^3 = 132651000$

$510^2 = 260100$

Square root of 26 = 5.10

6th October

6th October can be expressed as 6/10

$610 = 61 * 10$

610 is the 16th Fibonacci number

(The numbers are obtained by adding two numbers to get the next)

Series: 0, 1, 1, 2, 3, 5, 8, 13, 21, 34, 55, 89, 144, 233, 377, 610, ...

$610 = 24^2 + 24 + (2 * 4 + 2)$

7th October

7th October can be expressed as 7/10

$710 = 2 * 5 * (2 * 5 * 7 + 1)$

$710 = 26^2 + 26^1 + 2^1 + 6^1$

Cube of 710 forms a pattern of continuous odd numbers: 3, 5, 7, 9, 11

$710^3 = 357911000$

$710 = (6 * 5 * 4 * 3 * 2 * 1) - 10$

8th October

8th October can be expressed as 8/10

$810 = 81 * 10$

810 can be expressed using digits 1, 2, 3, 4 and 5

$810 = 1 * 2 * 3^4 * 5$

$1/810 = 0.123456789\%$

$810 = 28^2 + 28 - 2$

$810^2 = 656100$

If we add the digits: $6 + 5 + 6 + 1 + 0 + 0 = 018$

Which is reverse of 810

9th October

9th October can be expressed as 9/10

$910 = 91 * 10$

$910 = 30^2 + 3^2 + 3^0$

$910 = 2 * 5 * 7 * 13$ (product of 4 primes)

910 is a happy number

$9^2 + 1^2 + 0^2 = 82$

$8^2 + 2^2 = 68$

$6^2 + 8^2 = 100$

$1^2 + 0^2 + 0^2 = 1$

$910^2 = 828100$

If we add the digits: $8 + 2 + 8 + 1 + 0 + 0 = 19$

Which is reverse of 910

10th October

10th October can be expressed as 10/10

All digits are binary (0 and 1)

$1010 = 10^3 + 10^1$

$1010 = (5! - 4! + 3! - 2! + 1!) * 10$

Most of the clock ad display the time:

10:10

$1010 = 2^{10} - 2 - 10 - (1 + 0 + 1 + 0)$

Sqrt of 102 is 10.10

$1010^2 = 1020100$

$1010^3 = 1030301$

$1010^4 = 10406040100$

11th October

11th October can be expressed as 11/10

$1110 = 3 * 37 * 10$

$1110 = 33^2 + 3 * 7$

$1110 = 4^5 + 4^3 + 4^2 + 4^1 + 4^{1/2}$

$1/1110 = 0.09009009009009...\%$

$1110^2 = 1232100$

$1110^3 = 1367631000$

12th October

12th October can be expressed as 12/10

$1210 = 11^3 - 11^2 = 1331 - 121$

$1210 = 35^2 - 3 * 5 = 1225 - 15 = 1210$

$1210^2 = 1464100$

1464100 is palindrome

1210 is an amicable number. A pair of numbers x and y is called amicable if the sum of the proper divisors of either one is equal to the other.

1210 and 1184 is second such pair

Sum of divisors of 1210 is 1184 1 + 2 + 4 + 8 + 16 + 32 + 37 + 74 + 148 + 296 + 592 = 1184

Sum of divisors of 1184 is 1210 1 + 2 + 5 + 10 + 11 + 22 + 55 + 110 + 121 + 242 + 605 = 1210

13th October

13th October can be expressed as 13/10

1310 is Smallest number so that it and its neighbours are products of three distinct primes

1309 and 1311 are neighbours of 1310

$1309 = 7 * 11 * 17$

$1311 = 3 * 19 * 23$

$1310 = 37^2 - 37^0 - 3^2 - 7^2 = 1369 - 1 - 9 - 49$

1310 is concatenation of 6th prime (13) and 6th composite (10) number

14th October

14th October can be expressed as 14/10

$1410 = 2 * 3 * 5 * 47$

$1410 = 2 * 3 * 5 * (2^5 + 5^2)$

Product of 4 distinct prime numbers

If we add the divisors of 1410, we get consecutive digits – 3456

$1 + 2 + 3 + 5 + 6 + 10 + 15 + 30 + 47 + 94 + 141 + 235 + 282 + 470 + 705 + = 3456$

$1410 = 37^2 - 3^2 + 7^2 + 37^0 = 1369 - 9 + 49 + 1$

15th October

15th October can be expressed as 15/10

$1510 = 2 * 5^1 * (5^0 + 5^2 + 5^3) = 2 * 5 * 151$

1510 in base 10 = 10110000010 in base 2

$(1510)_{10} = (10110000010)_2$

$1 + 5 + 1 + 0 = 1 + 0 + 1 + 1 + 0 + 0 + 0 + 0 + 0 + 1 + 0 = 7$

16th October

16th October can be expressed as 16/10

$1610 = 2 * 5 * 7 * 23 = 2 * 5 * 7 * (2^5 - 7)$

$1610 = 40^2 + 4^2 - 4^1 - 4^{1/2}$

$1610 = 2 * 5 * 7 * (1^4 + 2^3 + 3^2 + 4^1 + 5^0)$

If we add the divisors of 1610, we get consecutive digits – 3456

$1 + 2 + 5 + 7 + 10 + 14 + 23 + 35 + 46 + 70 + 115 + 161 + 230 + 322 + 805 + 1610 = 3456$

1610 in base 10 = 11001001010

$(1610)_{10} = (11001001010)_2$

$1 + 6 + 1 + 0 = 1 + 1 + 0 + 0 + 1 + 0 + 0 + 1 + 0 + 1 + 0 = 8$

If we reverse 1510, we get 151 which is a prime number. Also 151 is one of the factors of 1510

17th October

17th October can be expressed as 17/10

Smallest non-palindrome where it and its reverse are divisible by 19

$1710/19 = 90$

$171/19 = 9$

First 5 digits of square root of 1710 contains 1, 2, 3, 4 and 5

$1710^{1/2} = 4.1352$

$1710 = 12^3 - (1 + 2) * (2 * 3)$

$1710 = 41^2 + (4 + 1)^2 + (4 * 1) = 1681 + 25 + 4$

18th October

18th October can be expressed as 18/10

1810 in base 10 = 24220 in base 5

$(1810)_{10} = (24220)_5$

1 + 8 + 1 + 0 = 2 + 4 + 2 + 2 + 0 = 10

If we reverse 1810, we get 181. 181 is prime. Also if we turn 181, upside down, 181 remains as 181

19th October

19th October can be expressed as 19/10

Sum of digits of the number, its square, its cube form a pattern of 11x

$1910^2 = 3648100$

$1910^3 = 6967871000$

1 + 9 + 1 + 0 = 11

3 + 6 + 4 + 8 + 1 + 0 + 0 = 22

6 + 9 + 6 + 7 + 8 + 7 + 1 + 0 + 0 + 0 = 44

$1910 = 2^{10} - 2^7 - 2^3 - 2^1 = 2048 - 128 - 8 - 2$

20th October

20th October can be expressed as 20/10

$2010 = 45^2 - 4^2 + 5^0 = 2025 - 16 + 1$

$2010 = 2^{10} - 10 * 2^2 + 2 = 2048 - 40 + 2$

$2010^2 = 4040100$

4040100 is a palindrome

October 20th is 294th day of the leap year

$2 * 9 * 4 = 72$

72, that's the number of days left in the year

21st October

21st October can be expressed as 21/10

$2110 = 2 * 5 * (3^5 - 2^5) = 2 * 5 * 211$

$2110 = 13^3 - 3 * 3^3 - 3 - 3 = 2197 - 81 - 6$

$2110 = 46^2 - [(4 + 6 + 2)/2] = 2116 - 6$

$2110 = 1 + 1 + 4 + 9 + 16 + 25 + 36 + 49 + 81 + 100 + 121 + 144 + 169 + 196 + 225 + 256 + 289 + 324$

It is one more than sum of squares of first 18 natural numbers

22nd October

22nd October can be expressed as 22/10

$2210 = 47^2 + 1^2$

$2210 = 43^2 + 19^2$

$2210 = 13 * 13 * 13 + 13 = 2197 + 13$

$2210 = 2 * (2 + 2 + 1) * 221$

$$2210 = {}_{47}C_2 + {}_{47}C_2 + {}_{47}C_1 + {}_{47}C_0$$

$$2210 = 47^2 - 4 + 7 - 2 = 2209 + 1$$

$$2210 = 41^2 + 23^2$$

$$2210 = 37^2 + 29^2$$

23rd October

23rd October can be expressed as 23/10

$$2310 = 2 * 3 * 5 * 7 * 11$$

It is product of first 5 prime numbers

The only 4-digit number to have this property; next is 30030 and previous is 210

$$2310 = 48^2 + 4^{1/2} + 8^{1/3} + 2^1 = 2304 + 2 + 2 + 2$$

$$2310 = (2 + 3 + 1 + 0) * 77$$

Both neighbours – 2309 and 23011 are prime numbers

24th October

24th October can be expressed as 24/10

$$2410 = 7^4 + (7 - 4)^2 = 2401 + 9$$

$$2410 = 49^2 + 3^2$$

$$2410 = 27^2 + 41^2$$

$$2410 = 2 * 5 * (170 + 071)$$

25th October

25th October can be expressed as 25/10

$2510 = 50^2 + 5 * 2$

The number of factors of 2510 = the number of factors formed by reversing its digits = 152

There are 8 factors of 2510 (1, 2, 5, 10, 251, 502, 1255, 2510) and there are 8 factors of 0152 (1, 2, 4, 8, 19, 38, 76, 152)

26th October

26th October can be expressed as 26/10

$2610 = 51^2 + 2 + 6 + 1 + 0$

$2610 = 51^2 + 3^2$

$2610 = 33^2 + 39^2$

$2610^2 = 6812100$

2610 is the only 4 digit number whose square consists of digits 0, 1, 2, 6 and 8

Both neighbours of 2610 – 2609 and 2611 are prime numbers

27th October

27th October can be expressed as 27/10

27th October is 300th day of non-leap year. 65 days remain for the year

$2710 = 52^2 + 52^0 = 2709 + 1$

$2710 = (2 + 7 + 1 + 0) * 271$

Square and Cube of 2710 when reversed are prime numbers

$2710^2 = 7344100 - \rightarrow$ Reversing 14437 is prime

$2710^3 = 19902511000 \rightarrow$ Reversing 11520991 is prime

28th October

28th October can be expressed as 28/10

$2810 = 53^2 + 53^0 = 2809 + 1$

$2810 = 43^2 + 31^2 = 1849 + 961$

Sum of digits of date = 2 + 8 gives 10 which is the month

$2810 = 7^4 + 7^3 + 7^2 + 7^1 + 10$

The prime factors of 2810 are 2, 5 and 281

Concatenation of 2, 5 and 281 gives the perfect square – $25281 = 159^2$

29th October

29th October can be expressed as 29/10

$2910 = 3 * 10^3 - 30 * 3 = 3000 - 90$

29 (birth date) is 10th (birth month) prime number

2910 is a Lucas-number

Start with "13", append sum of first 2 digits to the preceding number, drop first digit

13, 34, 47, 711, 118, 182, 829, 2910...

2910 in base 10 = 231132 in base 4

$(2910)_{10} = (231132)_4$

231132 is palindrome

30th October

30th October can be expressed as 30/10

3010 = 55 * 55 − 5 − 5 − 5

$3010^2 = 9060100$

If we revere 3010, we get 0103

$103^2 = 10609$ which is reverse of 90601

3010 is the number whose sum of digits is equal number of digits

3010 is a 4 (3 + 0 + 1 + 0) digit number

3010 = 2 * 5 * 7 * 43

Also 3010 is product of 4 (3 + 0 + 1 + 0) prime numbers

Alliterative numbers: Positive integers n such that all words in n's name begin with the same letter

3010 – Three Thousand & Thirty

Sum of cube of digits is sum of digits of cube

$3 + 0 + 1 + 0 = 4^3 = 64 = 6 + 4 = 10$

$3010^3 = 27270901000 = 10$ Digits

31st October

31st October can be expressed as 31/10

$3110 = 55 * 55 + 5^2 + 5^2 + 5^2 + 5 + 5$

$3110 = (3 + 1 + 1 + 0) * 622$

$3110 = 56^2 - 5^2 - 6^0 = 3136 - 25 - 1$

$3110 = (6^0 + 6^1 + 6^2 + 6^3 + 6^4) * (3 + 1 + 1 + 0)^{1/2}$

November

1st November can be expressed as 1/11

$111 = (1 + 1 + 1) * 37$

$111 = 16 + 17 + 18 + 19 + 20 + 21$

$111 = (1 + 2 + 3 + ... + 34 + 35 + 36) / 6$

$111 \times 111 = 12321$

$1111 \times 1111 = 1234321$

$11111 \times 11111 = 123454321$

$111111 \times 111111 = 12345654321$

$1111111 \times 1111111 = 1234567654321$

$11111111 \times 11111111 = 123456787654321$

$111111111 \times 111111111 = 12345678987654321$

111 is the smallest possible magic constant of a 3 x 3 magic square of distinct primes

67	1	43
13	37	61
31	73	7

2nd November

2nd November can be expressed as 2/11

$211 = 1 + 2 * 3 * 5 * 7$

$211 = (2 + 1)^5 - 2^5$

$211 = 6^3 - 6^1 + 6^0$

$211 = 15^2 - 15^1 + 15^0$

$211 = 14^2 + 14^1 + 14^0$

Both birthdate (2 -first one digit prime) and birth month (11 – first 2 digit prime) are prime

211 is the only 3 digit prime whose sum of any two digits is also prime

$2 + 1 = 3$ is prime

$1 + 1 = 2$ is prime

Cube of 211 consists of only 3 digits which are power of 3

$3^0 = 1, 3^1 = 3$ and $3^2 = 9$

$211^3 = 9393931$

3rd November

3rd November can be expressed as 3/11

311 is a prime number

If we reverse 311, 113 is also prime

Birth date 3 is prime and so is birth month – 11

131 is prime too

3 + 1 + 1 = 5 is prime

3 * 1 * 1 = 3 is prime

$3^2 + 1^2 + 1^2 = 11$ is prime

$3^3 + 1^3 + 1^3 = 29$ is prime

4th November

4th November can be expressed as 4/11

$411 = 20^2 + 2^0 + 2^1 + 2^3$

$411 = 19^2 + 19 * 2 + 1 + 9 + 2$

Drop any digit from 411 gives a prime

Drop 4, 11 remains

Drop 1, 41 remains

411 + 10 = 421 is prime

411 − 10 = 401 is prime

4 + 1 + 1 = 6 and the 6th letter is F. 411 Begins with F

Four Hundred & Eleven

5th November

5th November can be expressed as 5/11

$511 = 2^0 + 2^1 + 2^2 + 2^3 + 2^4 + 2^5 + 2^6 + 2^7$

$511 = 22 * 22 + 22 + 2 + 2 + 2^0$

$511 = 23^2 - 2 * 3 * 2$

$511 = 2^8 - 2^0$

$511 = 8^3 - 8^0$

$511 = (5 + 1 + 1) * (51 + 11 + 11)$

Both birth date and month are prime numbers

11 is the 5th prime number

6th November

6th November can be expressed as 6/11

$611 = [30 + (6 + 11)][30 - (6 + 11)] = (30 + 17)(30 - 17) = 900 - 289$

$611 = 25^2 - 2 * 5 - 2 * 2$

$611 = 24 * 24 + 24 + 2 * 4 + 2$

$611 = 5^3 * 2^2 + 5^2 * 2^2 + 5^1 * 2 + 5 * 2^0$

$6 + 11 = 17$ is prime

Drop any digit from 611, what remains is prime

Drop 6, 11 remains. 11 is prime

Drop 1, 61 remains. 61 is prime

7th November

7th November can be expressed as 7/11

$711 = 3^6 - 3 * 6$

$711 = (7 + 1 + 1)^3 - (7 + 1 + 1 - 3) * 3$

$711 = 26^2 + 26^1 + 26^0 + 2 + 6$

$711 = 27^2 - 27^1 + 2 + 7$

Both birth date and month are primes

$7 * 1 * 1 = 7$ is prime

Drop any digit from 711, what remains is prime

Drop 7, 11 remains. 11 is prime

Drop 1, 71 remains. 71 is prime

711 have only straight digits (1 and 7)

8th November

8th November can be expressed as 8/11

$811 = 9^2 + 10^2 + 11^2 + 12^2 + 13^2 + 14^2$

811 is a prime number

$8 + 11 = 17$ is prime

811 can be expressed as sum of 3 primes ending in 7

$811 = 7 + 797 + 7$

$811 = (27 + 1)^2 + 27$

Each digit of 811 is a perfect cube (8, 1 and 1 are perfect cube)

81 and 1 are perfect squares

9th November

9th November can be expressed as 9/11

The product of digits gives the birth months and the sum of digits gives birth date

9 * 1 * 1 = 9 – Birth date

9 + 1 + 1 = 11 – Birth Month

$9^2 + 1^2 + 1^2 = 81 + 1 + 1 = 83$ is prime

10th November

10th November can be expressed as 10/11

November 10 is the 314th day of the year (315th in leap years) in the Gregorian calendar

3.14 is the value of pi to two decimal places

$1011^2 = 1022121$

The square of 1011 is nothing but inserting three 2's in 1011

$1011 = 10^3 + 10^1 + 10^0$

$1111 = 6^4 - 6^3 + 6^2 - 6^1$

$1011 = 2^{10} - 2^3 - 2^2 - 2^1$

1011 = (1 + 0 + 1 + 1) * 337

11th November

11th November can be expressed as 11/11

1111 – Only date in DD-MM format to have all four same digits

Both birth date and birth month are prime

1111 can be expressed in the form $x^3 + x^2 + x^1 + x^0$

$1111 = 6^4 - 6^3 + 6^2 - 6^1 + 6^0$

$1111 = 10^3 + 10^2 + 10^1 + 10^0$

Square of 1111 is a palindrome

$1111^2 = 1234321$

1111 is a number whose sum of digits is equal to number of digits

$1 + 1 + 1 + 1 = 4$ and 1111 is a 4-digit number

There are 4 factors of 1111: 1, 11, 101 and 1111

All four are palindrome

$1111 = 11^2 + 12^2 + 13^2 + 14^2 + 152 + 16^2$

1111 is Strobogrammatic number: It remains the same when turned upside down

12th November

12th November can be expressed as 12/11

$1211 = 11^3 - 11^2 + 11^0$

$1211 = 35^2 + 35^0 - 3 * 5$

$1211 = 34^2 - 3^2 + 4^3$

$1211^2 = 1466521$

Let's reverse the number 1211 and let's see what happens to the square

$1121^2 = 1256641$

13th November

13th November can be expressed as 13/11

Both birth date and birth month are prime individually

13 and 11 are consecutive primes

$1311 = 36^2 + 3^2 + 6$

$1311 = 37^2 - 3^2 - 7^2$

$13 + 11 = 24 \rightarrow 4 * 3 * 2 * 1$

14th November

14th November can be expressed as 14/11

1411 is the number having only straight digits (1, 4 and 7)

At 14:11 (11 minutes past 2), the angle between minute hand and hour hand is almost 0 degrees

Number whose product of digits is equal to number of digits

$1 * 4 * 1 * 1 = 4$ and 1411 is a 4 digit number

15th November

15th November can be expressed as 15/11

1511 is prime number. The prime previous and next to 1511 is 1499 and 1523. Both are 12 away from 1511

$1 * 5 * 1 * 1 = 5$ is a prime number

1511 is the **largest** 4-digit number which is prime and whose product of digits is also 5

If we reverse 1511, we get 1151. 1151 is also prime

1511 can be expressed as sum of 3 consecutive primes

$1511 = 499 + 503 + 509$

1511 can be expressed as sum of 9 consecutive primes

$1511 = 149 + 151 + 157 + 163 + 167 + 173 + 179 + 181 + 191$

$1511 = 39^2 - 39^0 - 3 - 9$

16th November

16th November can be expressed as 16/11

$1611 = 40^2 + 4^2 - 4^1 - 4^0$

$1 * 6 * 1 * 6 = 6$

6 is the sum of digits when 1611 is written in base 2

1611 in base 10 = 11001001011 in base 2

The neighbour primes to 1611 are 1609 and 1613. Both are 2 away from 1611

$1611 = 81 + 82 + 83 + ... + 96$

17th November

17th November can be expressed as 17/11

1711 – Both birth date and birth months are prime numbers (17 and 11)

11 is the 5th prime number and 17 is 7th prime number. 5 and 7 are prime too

1711 is semi-prime as it can be written as product of two primes

1711 = 29 * 59

1711 is sum of first 58 natural numbers

1711 = 1 + 2 + 3 + 4 + ... + 58

18th November

18th November can be expressed as 18/11

1811 is a prime number

If we reverse 1811, we get 1181

1181 is prime too

1 + 1 + 8 + 1 = 11 is the prime number and also the birth month

18 + 11 = 29 is prime too

Each digit individually is a perfect cube: 1 and 8 both are perfect cubes

1811 = 42^2 + 42^1 + 4^1 + 2^0

19th November

19th November can be expressed as 19/11

1911 – Both birth date and birth months are prime numbers (19 and 11)

Square of 1911 begins with 365. That's the exact number of days in a non-leap year

Last 4 digits of the perfect square of 1911 is 1921

$1911^2 = 3651921$

$1911 = 43^2 + 4^3 - 4^{1/2}$

$1911 = 141 + 142 + 143 + ... + 153$

1911 has $1 + 9 + 1 + 1 = 12$ factors

20th November

20th November can be expressed as 20/11

2011 is a prime number

The year 1997, 1999, 2003 and 2007 are prime

The difference between

$1999 - 1197 = 2 = 2^1$

$2003 - 1999 = 4 = 2^2$

$2011 - 2003 = 8 = 2^3$

2011 can be express as sum of 11 consecutive primes

2011 = 157 + 163 + 167 + 173 + 179 + 181 + 191 + 193 + 197 + 199 + 211

The sum of digits of 2011 = 2 + 0 + 1 + 1 = 4 is equal to number of digits = 4

$2011^2 = 4044121$

If we reverse 2011, the square of it gets reversed

$1102^2 = 1214404$

21st November

21st November can be expressed as 21/11

2111 is a prime number

2 * 1 * 1 * 1 = 2 is prime

2 + 1 + 1 + 1 = 5 is prime

The two neighbour primes to 2111 are 2109 and 2103. Both are 2 away from it

If we reverse 2111 and add it to 2111 we get 3223 which is palindrome

If we reverse 2111 and subtract it from 2111, we get 999 which is palindrome

If we reverse 2111 and multiply it with 2111, we get 2347432 which is palindrome

If we divide 2111 in two parts: 211 and 1 and add them, we get 212 which is palindrome

Square of 2111 consists of digits: 1, 2, 3, 4, 5 and 6

$2111^2 = 4456321$

If we reverse 2111, we get 1112. By squaring 1112 we get the reverse square of 2111

$1112^2 = 1236544$

22nd November

22nd November can be expressed as 22/11

The birth date is twice the value of birth month

$2211 - 1122 = 33^2 = 1089$

2211 is sum of first $(2 + 2 + 1 + 1) * 11 = 66$ natural numbers

$2211 = 1 + 2 + 3 + ... + 66$

$2211 = 47^2 + 47^0 + 47^0$

$2211^2 = 488521$

If we reverse 2211, the square also gets reversed

$1122^2 = 125884$

23rd November

23rd November can be expressed as 23/11

2311 Both birth month and birth date are prime

2311 is prime number

$2 + 3 + 1 + 1 = 7$ is prime too

Cube root of 2311 consists of digits 1, 2 and 3

$2311^{1/3} = 13.22$

$2311 = 48^2 + 48^0 + 4^1 + 8^{1/3}$

24th November

24th November can be expressed as 24/11

2411 is the number whose product of digits = sum of its digits

$2 * 4 * 1 * 1 = 2 + 4 + 1 + 1$

Each digit can be expressed as power of 2

$2 = 2^1, 4 = 2^2$ and $1 = 2^0$

$2411 = 49^2 + 2 * (4^{1/2} + 9^{1/2})$

25th November

25th November can be expressed as 25/11

2511 is a prime number

2511 has $2 * 5 * 1 * 1 = 10$ factors

$2511 = 66 + 67 + 68 + ... + 96$

25th November is 329th day of the non-leap year. Exact 36 days remain until the end of the year

$36 = 25 + 11$

$2511 = 50^2 + 50^1 + 5 * 2$

$2511 = 50^2 + 11$

26th November

26th November can be expressed as 26/11

$2611 - (2 + 6 + 1 + 1) = 2601 = 51^2$

$2611 = 180 + 181 + 182 + ... + 193$

2611 in base 10 = 101000110011 in base 2

$(2611)_{10} = (101000110011)_2$

2611 is digitally balanced number in base 2 as it contains equal number of 1's and 0's

27th November

27th November can be expressed as 27/11

2711 is a prime number

$2 + 7 + 1 + 1 = 11$ is a prime number

2711 is concatenation of 3 primes: 2, 7 and 11

The internal digits of 2711 i.e. 71 is prime

$2711^{10} - 2711^9 - 2711^8 - 2711^7 - 2711^6 - 2711^5 - 2711^4 - 2711^3 - 2711^2 - 2711 - 1$ is prime

$2711 = 52^2 + 5^1 + 2^1$

28th November

28th November can be expressed as 28/11

28th November is 333rd day of the leap year starting from 1st January

31st Dec is just 33 days far from 28th November

2811 Each digit of 2811 can be expressed in power of 2

$2 = 2^1, 8 = 2^3$ and $1 = 2^0$

$2811 - 8 = 2803$ is prime

$2811 + 8 = 2819$ is prime

$2811 = 53^2 + 5^0 + 3^0$

Drop any digit of 2811 and what remains is prime

Drop 2. 811 is prime

Drop 8. 211 is prime

Drop 1. 281 is prime

29th November

29th November can be expressed as 29/11

29th November is 333rd day of non-leap year starting from 1st January

Exact 33 days remains for the year (31st Dec) including 29th November

Both 29 and 11 are primes

$2 + 9 + 1 + 1 = 13$ is prime

Sum of factors of 2911 − 1 and 2911 + 1 are same

Sum of all factors of 2910 is 7056

Sum of all factors of 2912 is 7056

2911 = 54 * 54 − 5

2911 = 6 + 7 + 8 + ... + 76

30th November

30th November can be expressed as 30/11

3011 is the largest date in DD-MM form which remains prime when read forward or backward

3011 is a prime number

If we reverse 3011 to get 1103. 1103 is prime too

3 + 0 + 1 + 1 = 5 is prime

3 * 1 * 1 = 3 is prime

30 + 11 = 41 is prime

If we re-arrange 3011, to get 1103. 1103 is prime too

Cube root of 3011 is 14.44

14.44 is perfect square of 3.8

3011^2 = 9066121

If we reverse LHS, RHS gets reversed

1103^2 = 1216609

December

1st December

1st December can be expressed as 1/12

$112 = 1 * 2 + 2 * 3 + 3 * 4 + 4 * 5 + 5 * 6 + 6 * 7$

$112 = 11^2 - 11 + 2$

$112 = (1 + 1)^7 - 2^4$

112 can be expressed as sum of 6 consecutive primes starting from 11

$112 = 11 + 13 + 17 + 19 + 23 + 29$

$112^2 = 12544$

$211^2 = 44521$

2nd December

2nd December can be expressed as 2/12

Square of 212 is palindrome with all 5 digits consists of only 4 and 9 which are individually perfect squares

Also 4 out of 5 digits is 4

$212^2 = 44944$

$212 = (2 + 12)^2 + 2^{(2 + 2)} = 14^2 + 4^2$

212 Degree Fahrenheit = 100 Degree Celsius (Boiling point of water)

3rd December

3rd December can be expressed as 3/12

Sum of digits = product of digits

$3 + 1 + 2 = 3 * 1 * 2 = 6$

$312 = 7^3 - 7 * 3 - 7 - 3$

$312 = 2 * 5^3 + 2 * 5^2 + 2 * 5^1 + 2 * 5^0$

$312 = 2^3 * 3 * 13$

Cube root of 312 is 6.78

4th December

4th December can be expressed as 4/12

412 contains digits which individually expressed as power of 2

$4 = 2^2, 1 = 2^0$ and $2 = 2^1$

412 can be expressed as sum of 4 * (1 + 2) = 12 consecutive primes

$412 = 13 + 17 + 19 + 23 + 29 + 31 + 37 + 41 + 43 + 47 + 53 + 59$

412 can be expressed as sum of consecutive natural numbers starting from 4 * 12 = 48

$412 = 48 + 49 + 50 + 51 + 52 + 53 + 54 + 55$

$412 = 21^2 - 21^1 - 2^{(2 + 1)}$

5th December

5th December can be expressed as 5/12

512 is a Dudeney number. Number which can be expressed as cube of sum of its digits

5 + 1 + 2 = 8 and 512 = 8 * 8 * 8

$512 = (5 + 1 + 2)^3 = 8^3$

If we rearrange 512, we get another perfect cube

$125 = 5^3$

512 can be expressed as $x^y + y^x$ (Leyland number)

$512 = 4^4 + 4^4$

$512 = 2^9$

$512 = 22^2 + 22 + 2 + 2 + 2$

6th December

6th December can be expressed as 6/12

612 has 6 + 12 = 18 factors

$612 = (12 * 2)^2 + (12/2)^2$

$612 = 24^2 + 24^1 + 24/2$

Square and cube of 612 consists of different digits

$612^2 = 374544$

$612^3 = 46225$

If we reverse the digits of 612, we get the perfect cube

$216 = 6^3$

The product of birth date and birth month gives 6 * 12 = 72

The Rule of 72 is a simple way to determine how long an investment will take to double given a fixed annual rate of interest

At 2% rate of interest, it takes 36 years (approximately)

At 3%, it takes 24 years (approximately)

At 6%, 12 years and so on...

7th December

7th December can be expressed as 7/12

$712 = 26^2 + 6^2$

If we rearrange 712, we get 127

$127 = 2^7 - 1$

712 is sum of first 21 prime numbers

$712 = 2 + 3 + 5 + ... + 73$

$712 = 27^2 - 27^0 - 2 * 7 - 2$

Largest number known that does not have any digits in common with its 8th power

$712^8 = 66,045,000,696,445,844,586,496$

The major and minor angles between minute and hour hand at 12 minutes past 7 is perfect cube and perfect square respectively

Major angle = $216 = 6^3$

Minor angle = $144 = 12^2$

8th December

8th December can be expressed as 8/12

$812 = 28 * (28 + 1)$

$812 = 29^2 - 29$

$812 = 28^2 + 28$

812 can be expressed as power of 2 individually

$8 = 2^3, 1 = 2^0$ and $2 = 2^1$

$8 * 1 * 2 = 16 = 2^4$

If we rearrange the digits of 812, we get 128

$128 = 2^{1 * 8}$

9th December

9th December can be expressed as 9/12

$912 = 9 + 1 + 2 + 30^2$

$9 * 1 * 2 =$ sqrt of $9/2 [9 + 1 + 2]$

Sum of four consecutive primes

$912 = 223 + 227 + 229 + 233$

Sum of ten consecutive primes

$912 = 71 + 73 + 79 + 83 + 89 + 97 + 101 + 103 + 107 + 109$

10th December

10th December can be expressed as 10/12

Insert three 4's in 1012 to get it's square

$1012^2 = 1024144$

$1012 = 2^{10} - 12$

$1012 = 32^2 - 3 * 2 * 2$

$2101 - 1012 = 1089 = 33^2$

1012 is sum of consecutive numbers from 33 to 55

$1012 = 33 + 34 + 35 ... + 55$

Sum of digits of 1012 = 1 + 0 + 1 + 2 = 4 = Number of digits of 1012 = 4

11th December

11th December can be expressed as 11/12

1112 when converted to base 3 starts with 1112

1112 in base 10 = 1112012

$(1112)_{10} = (1112012)_3$

1112 is the sum of two prime numbers in 16 different ways, the fewest for any four-digit even number

1112, when reverse becomes prime. 2111 is prime

$1112 = 33 * (33 + 1)$

Square root of 1112 is 33.3

Square of 1112 consists of digits 1, 2, 3, 4, 5 and 6

$1112^2 = 1236544$

Reverse LHS to get RHS reversed

$2111^2 = 4456321$

12th December

12th December can be expressed as 12/12

1212 has 12 factors

1212 when divided by 12 gives first three-digit prime 101

$1212^2 = 1468944$

Reverse LHS to get RHS reversed

$2121^2 = 4498641$

$12 + 12 = 24 = 4! = 4 * 3 * 2 * 1$

Product of digits = Number of digits

$1 * 2 * 1 * 2 = 4 = $ Number of digits of 1212

$1212 = 35^2 - 3 - 5 * 2$

1212 can be expressed as sum of 12 consecutive primes

$1212 = 73 + 79 + 83 + ... + 131$

13th December

13th December can be expressed as 13/12

$1312 = 36^2 + 4^2$

$1312 = 2^4 + 6^4$

The major and minor angle formed between minute and hour hands at 12 minutes passed 13 hours are perfect squares

Major Angle = $324 = 18^2$

Minor Angle = $36 = 6^2$

14th December

14th December can be expressed as 14/12

$14 * 12 = 168$

That's the numbers of hours in a week ($24 * 7 = 168$)

Cube of 1412 is special as the digits of its cube occur with same frequency

$1412^3 = 2815166528$

We have two 1's, 2's, 5's, 6's and 8's

Product of digits = sum of digits

$1 * 4 * 1 * 2 = 1 + 4 + 1 + 2$

$1412 = 34^2 + 16^2$

$1412 = 38^2 - 3 * 8 - 8$

$2141 - 1412 = 729 = 27^2 = 9^3 = 3^7$

15th December

15th December can be expressed as 15/12

$1512 = 6^3 + 6^4$

Cube of 1512 begins with 3456...

$1512^3 = 3456649728$

$1512 = 39^2 - 3^2$

If we rearrange last 2 digits of 1512, we get perfect square

$1521 = 39^2$

16th December

16th December can be expressed as 16/12

$1612 = 1 * 2 + 3 + 4 * 5 + 6 + 7 * 8 + 9 + 10 * 11 + 12 + 13 * 14 + 15 + 16 * 17 + 18 + 19 * 20 + 21 + 22 * 23$

$1612 = 39^2 + 39^0 + 3^2 + 9^2$

1612 Sum of birth date and birth month is a perfect number – 28

28 can be expressed as sum of its factors (excluding 28)

$28 = 1 + 2 + 4 + 7 + 14$

16th December is 350th day of non-leap year starting from 1st January. Exact 16 days to go for the remaining year (31st Dec)

$1612 - 12 = 1600 = 40^2$

1612 has 12 factors

17th December

17th December can be expressed as 17/12

1 + 7 + 1 + 2 = 11 is a prime number

17 + 12 = 29 is a prime number

17 is prime number

1712 is concatenation of 7th prime number (17) and 7th composite (12) number

$1712 = 12^3 - 17 - 1$

$1712 = 42^2 - 42^1 - 4 * 2 - 2$

A cake can be cut into 1712 by 58 [2 * (17 + 12)] straight cuts

18th December

18th December can be expressed as 18/12

$1812 = 18 * 12 = 216 = (18 - 12)^3$

Each digit individually consists of power of 2

$1 = 2^0, 8 = 2^3$ and $2 = 2^1$

$1812 = 64 + 65 + 66 + ... + 87$

19th December

19th December can be expressed as 19/12

$1912 = 44 * 44 - 4!$

$1912 = 43^2 + 4^3 - 3^0$

Square of 1912 consist of consecutive digits 3, 4, 5, 6 and 7

$1912^2 = 3655744$

19 + 12 = 31 is prime

1 + 9 + 1 + 2 = 13 is prime

20th December

20th December can be expressed as 20/12

$20 + 12 = 32 = 2^5 = 2^{(2 + 0 + 1 + 2)}$

$2012^2 = 4048144$

Reverse LHS to get RHS reversed

$2102^2 = 4418404$

2012 is the first year in which February had 5 Wednesdays

2012 Consists of first 3 digits: 0, 1, 2

21st December

21st December can be expressed as 21/12

2112 is palindrome

2112 is sandwiched between two primes: 2111 and 2113

$2112 = 2^{11} + 2^{(2 + 1 + 1 + 2)}$

$2112 = 46^2 + 2^2$

$2112 = 13 * 13 * 13 - 13 - 13 - 13 - 13 - 13$

Products of digits = Number of digits

$2 * 1 * 1 * 2 = 4$ = Number of digits of 2112

2112 remains the same when turned upside down (using calculator-style numerals)

2112 is the first year of 22nd century to have 5 Mondays in February

22nd December

22nd December can be expressed as 22/12

2212 closest integer to 17^e

A cake can be cut into 2212 pieces by using only 66 straight cuts

$2212 = 47^2 + 7 - 4$

$2212 = 13^3 + 13^1 + 1^0 + 3^0$

$2212 = 12 + 13 + 14 + ... + 67$

The major angle between minute hand and hour hand at 12 past 22 hours is 234

23rd December

23rd December can be expressed as 23/12

$2312 = 2 + 3 + 1 + 2 + 48^2$

$2312 = 2 * 34^2$

Square of 2312 consists of 3 consecutive digits: 3, 4 and 5 and exhibits pattern: 534

$2312^2 = 5345344$

Sum of cube of digits is sum of digits of cube

Sum of Cube of Digits = 8 + 27 + 1 + 8 = 44

Sum of Digits of Cube = 12358435328 = 1 + 2 + 3 + 5 + 8 + 4 + 3 + 5 + 3 + 2 + 8 = 44

2312 can be expressed as sum starting from 2^8 till 12^2

2312 = 128 + 129 + 130 + ... + 144

24th December

24th December can be expressed as 24/12

2 + 4 + 1 + 2 = 9 is a perfect square

2 * 4 * 1 * 2 = 16 is a perfect square

24 + 12 = 36 is a perfect square

241 + 2 = 243 is perfect 5th power of 3

$2412 = 49^2 + 9 + 2$

Sum of cubes of the digits equals the square of the sum of the digits

Sum of cube of 2412 = 8 + 64 + 1 + 8 = 81

Square of Sum of digits = 2 + 4 + 1 + 2 = 9 and $9^2 = 81$

2412 is a leap year

25th December

25th December can be expressed as 25/12

2512 is the smallest number whose 5th power has 17 digits

6th power of 2512 starts with 2512

$2516^6 = 2512...$

$2512 = 50^2 + 2 * 5 + 2$

$2512 = 24 * 24 + 44 * 44$

Product of digits is twice the sum of digits

$2 * 5 * 1 * 2 = 2 * (2 + 5 + 1 + 2)$

26th December

26th December can be expressed as 26/12

$2612 = 26 * 26 + 44 * 44$

$2 * 6 * 1 * 2 = 4! = 4 * 3 * 2 * 1$

$2612 = 51^2 + 5 * 2 + 1$

$2612 = 3 * 30^2 - 3 * 30 - 2$

27th December

27th December can be expressed as 27/12

2712 can be expressed using digits 1, 2, 3, 4 and 5

$2712 = 14^3 - 2^5 = 2744 - 32$

$2712 = 52^2 + 5 - 2$

Product of digits gives a perfect number

2 * 7 * 1 * 2 = 28

28 can be expressed as sum of its factors (Excluding self)

28 = 1 + 2 + 4 + 7 + 14

28th December

28th December can be expressed as 28/12

2812 Each digit can be expressed as powers of 2 individually

$2 = 2^1$, $8 = 2^3$ and $1 = 2^0$

$2 * 8 * 1 * 2 = 32 = 2^{(8-2-1)} = 2^5$

$2812 = 53^2 + 3^1$

2812 = 2500 + 250 + 50 + 5 + 5 + 2

29th December

29th December can be expressed as 29/12

2912 can be expressed using prime numbers 2, 5, 7, and 13

$2912 = 2^5 * 7 * 13$

$2912 = 54^2 - 4$

2 + 9 + 1 + 2 = 14

29 + 12 = 41

$2 * 9 * 1 * 2 = 36 = 6^2$

Year 2012 have five Mondays in the month of February

30th December

30th December can be expressed as 30/12

$3012 = 35^2 - 3 * 5 - 3 + 5$

Factors of 3012 are

1, 2, 3, 4, 6, 12, 251, 502, 753, 1004, 1506, 3012

☻ if we take factors containing only digit 5 and add them, we get 3012

$3012 = 251 + 502 + 753 + 1506$

3012 represents an analog clock with 30 degrees * 12 hours to give 360 degrees

Sum of digits = product of non-zero digits

$3 + 0 + 1 + 2 = 3 * 1 * 2 = 6$

3012 consists of first 4 digits: 0, 1, 2 and 3 and can be expressed using digits 1, 2, 3, 4 and 5

$3012 = 251 * 3 * 4$

Cube root of 3012 is 14.44

14.44 is a perfect square of 3.8

31st December

31st December can be expressed as 31/12

31st December is 365th day in a non-leap year

365 is the smallest number which can be expressed as sum of consecutive squares in two ways

$365 = 10^2 + 11^2 + 12^2$

31st Dec is 366th day in a leap year

$366 = 8^2 + 9^2 + 10^2 + 11^2$

$365 = 13^2 + 14^2$

$3112 = 2 * (6^0 + 6^1 + 6^2 + 6^3 + 6^4) + 2$

$3112 = 56^2 - 5 * 6 + 6$

$3112 = 54^2 + 14^2$

Sum of cube of digits of 3112 is sum of digits of cube of 3112

Sum of cube of digits of 3112 = 27 + 1 + 1 + 8 = 37

Sum of digits of cube of 3112 = 30138300928 = 3 + 0 + 1 + 3 + 8 + 3 + 0 + 0 + 9 + 2 + 8 = 37

Reference

The On-line Encyclopedia of Integer Sequences (OEIS)

Numbers – Wikipedia

NCERT – Class X, IX and X

Quantitative Aptitude by Arun Sharma

Note

A special thanks to Indrani Cs for the finishing touches she gave to this book.

Manufactured by Amazon.ca
Bolton, ON

15211714R00143